The IEA Health and Welfare Unit

Choice in Welfare No. 19

Liberating Women ...
From Modern Feminism

D1392127

Two week
loan

Please return on or before the last
date stamped below.
Charges are made for late return.

The IEA Health and Welfare Unit

Choice in Welfare No. 19

Liberating Women ...
From Modern Feminism

Norman Barry
Mary Kenny
Michael Levin
Patricia Morgan
Joan Kennedy Taylor
Glenn Wilson

Caroline Quest (Editor)

IEA Health and Welfare Unit
London, 1994

First published March 1994

The IEA Health and Welfare Unit
2 Lord North St
London SW1P 3LB

© The IEA Health and Welfare Unit 1994

ISBN 0-255 36353-2

Typeset by the IEA Health and Welfare Unit
in Palatino 11 on 12 point
Printed in Great Britain by
Goron Pro-Print Co. Ltd
Churchill Industrial Estate, Lancing, West Sussex

Contents

Foreword

There is a tendency to think of feminism as a single movement representing the interests of all women. Indeed, as a general rule, the more extreme the opinion, the more likely it is to be represented as embodying the true interests of all women. But there are several feminist schools of thought, some of which are compatible with a free society and some not. Two particular doctrines are not compatible with liberty: 'quota feminism' and 'anti-family feminism'.

One of the increasing pressures on company managers is the demand for recruitment and promotion policies to discriminate in favour of female employees. Sometimes the rationale behind this demand is that women have suffered historic wrongs which need to be rectified, and on other occasions the reasoning is that women and men should be equally represented at all levels in any organisation, and especially at the top. Managers who are trying to maintain a policy of recruitment and promotion according to merit are having an increasingly hard time.

The power of the modern demand for reverse discrimination rests on the use of language which implies equality of opportunity, when its real aim is parity of outcome. Feminists at the end of the nineteenth century and earlier this century sought equality of opportunity. They recognised that there were fundamental differences between men and women, both genetic and cultural, and that it was both inevitable and desirable that males and females would play different roles. Their hope was that people should be treated as individuals, according to their own merits, and not according to their gender category. Consequently, they campaigned for the removal of barriers to allow women to compete on merit. For example, they urged that careers in medicine or law should not be barred to women and that females should not be forced to resign from work when they married, as required of female civil servants at one time. Their objection was to the treatment of women, *merely*, as members of a category; their demand was that women should be treated as morally responsible individuals, who should be given a chance to prove their worth.

Many modern radical feminists have entirely reversed the argument, whilst continuing to use the language of opportunity.

They argue that women are, above all, members of the female gender category, and proceed to demand that they should be given special privileges, not on merit, but as females. To argue in this manner reduces women to the status of victims who cannot make it on their own.

What makes us human is that we are thinking, valuing individuals endowed with a sense of personal moral responsibility and a capacity to improve the world around us. 'Quota feminists' diminish women by treating them as the 'replaceable' members of a category, not as uniquely endowed potential contributors to human advance.

Radical post-1960s feminism has also diminished women in another fundamental sense. Some extreme feminists take the view that marriage is a condition in which women are dependent on men and urge females to become independent of men through work, and some even take the view that it is better to be dependent on state welfare benefits than to rely on a man's income. As Professor Barry's thoughtful essay in this collection shows, marriage is not a relationship involving one-sided dependency. It is a binding agreement, binding equally on both male and female, to support each other and the children of the union. Its value is that we voluntarily enter into a condition which binds us to our enlightened long-term interests, by protecting us from the passing passions and fancies which may distract us during the course of a lifetime.

Consider the consequences of being liberated from the 'dominance' of a man for never-married lone mothers, struggling to bring up children single-handed with no more than welfare benefits to rely on. In what sense are they liberated? In practice, it is the absconding fathers of their children who have been liberated from taking responsibility for their own offspring. Past generations of women, and especially feminists, have insisted that men must share the responsibility for raising children. Today's message, however, is that men are free to sire babies at will and that their obligation is completed after copulation. Women are not being liberated by this doctrine, they are being left to cope alone, at a high cost to their own quality of life and that of their children.

Why are quota feminism and anti-family feminism incompatible with liberty? Liberty is a social ideal which rests on self-imposed restraint in preference to externally imposed control. It rests, as Acton understood, on conscience, nurtured in youth and affirmed in adulthood in the face of the challenges and temptations of daily living. Liberty is an ideal designed for people who walk the streets guided by a moral compass.

The family is fundamental to a free society because it is where men and women acquire the virtues which make liberty workable. Personal freedom for all in a complex and diverse modern society is only possible if we seek to live up to the ideal of personal responsibility, which inevitably means free acceptance of self-imposed restraint for our own good and that of others. Anti-family feminism and quota feminism are not consistent with this ethos. Quota feminism implies a coercive state apportioning jobs by fiat and anti-family feminism promotes a narrow, selfish individualism, which is harmful, above all, to children. Both doctrines see women as victims. Quota feminism sees women as permanent victims who must be compensated in the jobs market with easy options; and anti-family feminism views marriage as a state in which women are the victims of men.

Some feminist campaigns have been compatible with freedom. For instance, the police should certainly protect women from violent partners, whether they are attacked in their own home or not. Any woman who wants to compete in traditional male preserves should be free to do so. And careers for women are not necessarily inconsistent with motherhood, particularly once the children start to attend school. Relationships within marriage have become more equal in the last century, and rightly so.

But 'quota feminism' and 'anti-family feminism' are very different doctrines from the earlier 'opportunity feminism'. Above all, they are not based on the sense of personal responsibility and consideration for others which is inseparable from real liberation. Hence the title of this collection: *Liberating Women ... From Modern Feminism*.

David G. Green

The Authors

Professor Norman Barry came to Buckingham in 1983 as Reader in Politics. He has been Professor of Politics since 1984. Previously he was Senior Lecturer in Government at the City of Birmingham Polytechnic (now the University of Central England). He specialises in social and political theory and his books include *Hayek's Social and Economic Philosophy*, 1979; *An Introduction to Modern Political Theory*, 1981 and 1989; *Welfare*, 1990 and *The Morality of Business Enterprise*, 1991. He has contributed to many periodicals and learned journals. He was Visiting Scholar at the Social Philosophy and Policy Centre, Bowling Green State University, Ohio. Professor Barry is a member of the Academic Advisory Councils of the Institute of Economic Affairs (London) and the David Hume Institute (Edinburgh).

Mary Kenny is a leading columnist for *The Sunday Telegraph* where she writes about matters of social interest, with particular focus on the history and politics of the family. She also contributes to the *Daily Mail*, the *Evening Standard*, the *Irish Independent* in Dublin and the weekly Catholic publication, *The Tablet*. She is a frequent broadcaster on radio and television. In the early 1970s she was involved in launching a feminist movement in Dublin while editing the woman's page of a national Irish newspaper. Subsequently she became features editor of the *Evening Standard* and then European correspondent.

Mary Kenny has published books about working mothers, about religion and about abortion. She has also published some short fiction.

Professor Michael Levin teaches philosophy at the City College and Graduate Centre of the City University of New York. He is the author of *Metaphysics and the Mind-Body Problem*, 1979 and *Feminism and Freedom*, 1987. He has published extensively in the technical areas of philosophy, primarily philosophy of science and foundations of logic and mathematics. He has also written extensively about feminism, race relations, and equal opportunity.

Patricia Morgan, Senior Research Fellow at the IEA's Health and Welfare Unit, is a sociologist specialising in criminology and family policy. She is the author or co-author of a number of books including: *Delinquent Phantasies*, 1978; *Facing Up to Family Income*, 1989; *The Hidden Costs of Childcare*, 1992 and *Families in Dreamland*, 1992. She has also contributed to many essay collections, periodicals and national newspapers. Patricia Morgan is a frequent contributor to television and radio programmes and is presently writing a full-length work on the relationship between capitalism and the family. She held the Morris Finer Research Scholarship at the London School of Economics.

Joan Kennedy Taylor is the author of *Reclaiming the Mainstream: Individualist Feminism Rediscovered*, 1992. She has directed book programmes for the Manhattan Institute and the Foundation for Economic Education; was an editor for *The Libertarian Review* and *The Freeman*; has written for US publications including *Reason*, *The Wall Street Journal*, and *Success* magazine; and contributed to the books *Freedom, Feminism, and the State*, 1982; *Beyond the Status Quo: Policy Proposals for America*, 1985 and *Equal Opportunities: A Feminist Fallacy*, 1992. She is the National Co-ordinator of the US Association of Libertarian Feminists.

Dr Glenn Wilson is a Senior Lecturer in Psychology at the Institute of Psychiatry, University of London. An expert on human sexual behaviour, he has published more than 200 scientific articles and over 20 books including *The Psychology of Sex*, 1979, with H.J. Eysenck; *Sexual Variations*, 1980; *Love and Instinct*, 1981 and *The Great Sex Divide*, 1989. He makes frequent radio and television appearances and has lectured widely abroad, holding visiting appointments at California State University, Los Angeles, Stanford University and The University of Nevada, Reno. Dr Wilson is a Fellow of the British Psychological Society.

Caroline Quest is currently Associate Editor at the IEA Health and Welfare Unit which she joined in 1987. She is co-author of *Competing for the Disabled*, 1989, (with C.S.B. Galasko) and editor of *Equal Opportunities: A Feminist Fallacy*, 1992. As well as women's issues, she has a particular interest in health care. She is married with two small children.

Editor's Introduction

Caroline Quest

Feminism is taken to be the voice of women. It calls itself the women's movement and is understood by officials and the public to be just that. Any criticism of feminism or its causes is viewed as an attack on women. It is not surprising therefore that feminism has managed largely to avoid critical scrutiny. Any criticisms that are made of feminism are merely dismissed as right-wing anger and discomfort about changing sex-roles. Feminists never deal with the substance of the criticisms, instead they tend to launch into a personal attack on the critic. Susan Faludi, author of the best-seller *Backlash*,[1] is an example. She takes less than a page to outline the central tenets of Professor Levin's devastating critique of feminism, *Feminism and Freedom*,[2] and over three pages to recall her observations of the way his family behaved during her interview with him. This is not critical debate. It is avoiding it.

Naomi Wolf, feminism's latest heroine, similarly manages to avoid tackling the substance of criticisms against feminism.[3] She restricts most of her analysis to differences within the feminist movement itself. Wolf argues that women who refuse to call themselves feminists are merely reacting to the outdated 'victim' feminism of the 1960s or the distorted image of feminism presented by the media. The conclusion to be drawn is that the majority of women do not call themselves feminists because they do not understand what feminism is and what it could do for them. If they knew what feminism was *really* about then they would be bound to be feminists.

Wolf's mission is to convert the non-identifying. She attempts this by creating 'power' feminism and demonstrating its relevance to the everyday lives of mainstream women. Breaking away from the drab, marginal, victim feminism, the 'competitive' and 'sexy' power feminism will use 'money, votes and social embarrassment' to fight the opposition.

Not surprisingly, power feminism ends up having as little relevance to most women as the victim feminism it is directed against. Although a wordy eighteen chapters, *Fire with Fire* has almost nothing to say about marriage, the family, motherhood, childcare, or working mothers, other than a few platitudes about dual parenting. The realities of combining a powerful position at work with being a good wife and mother go virtually undiscussed. The free choice of many women to sacrifice their career, or at least to severely interrupt it, in order to raise a family and willingly become dependent upon their partner, seems incompatible with Wolf's feminism. Power feminism is for pre-maternal young women; it is of little relevance and help to the realities of life for the majority of real women.

The emergence in recent years of 'establishment feminists' who occupy influential positions within the media and government makes it even more important for critical debate to take place. Such a debate is what the present collection provides. Each author discusses an issue of particular concern to women today from a frame of reference that is sharply divergent from and critical of contemporary feminist thinking.

According to the first author, Patricia Morgan, the mass entry of women into the labour force—both encouraged by government tax and employment policies as well as campaigned for by feminists—has resulted in a living standard based on two incomes. This two-income norm is now adversely affecting the ability of couples to start a family. This is because it makes raising a family an expensive use of women's time in terms of earnings foregone. The lowering of tax thresholds to hit one-income families hardest as well as the inflexibility of the wage structure caused by equal opportunities legislation are restricting the ability of women to strike a balance between work and family life.

For Morgan, the feminist solution to these problems—state-funded childcare—will further drive up the costs for mothers of staying at home which will become an unaffordable option for most women. Families, and in particular children, will suffer from the increase in stress, fatigue, and decline in parental attention that are all associated with dual-earner families. Women's occupational advancement would not necessarily be jeopardised by the restoration of the family economy through family tax allowances and flexible pay policies.

The purpose of Mary Kenny's essay is to examine the feminist proposition that women are disadvantaged relative to men by the traditional 'patriarchal' family. She suggests that this is far from being the reality which is rather that the family is a matriarchal institution. Kenny observes that the contemporary feminist view that marriage serves only men and 'exploitative capitalism' is enormously influential. She estimates that millions of women have acted on these anti-family views which have contributed to the demise of conventional marriage and family life. However, by appealing to historical and contemporary evidence, Kenny argues that the family serves women too. It does this by providing a power-base for women to fulfil their desires for motherhood, relationships with kin, and even the development of the feminine personality. The tearing down of the patriarchal family has, therefore, been misguided; it has not resulted in women's liberation but in crime, poverty, and social dislocation.

In 'Justice and Liberty in Marriage and Divorce,' Professor Norman Barry calls for the liberal concept of justice to be applied to the dissolution of marriage. This, he argues, would provide the pre-commitment which is essential if the stability of the family is to be restored. It would entail fully restoring fault to the system of marital law and is precisely the opposite of what is being proposed in the Lord Chancellor's Green Paper. According to Barry, today's marriage laws have perverted the moral ideal of liberty based on the idea of personal responsibility for action. This is because the state has taken on the costs that accrue when individuals make mistakes. The result has been a rise in one-parent families, permissiveness, and divorce. According to Barry, marriage laws should recognise that the marriage contract creates rights and duties which must be respected. Only these could provide the elements of pre-commitment which morally vulnerable men and women require to avoid doing themselves long-term harm. Therefore, if fidelity is a duty of marriage, then it would be just that spouses 'pay' for being unfaithful.

Fully restoring fault to marital law would be more beneficial to women than using marital law, for which feminists have argued, as a device for equalising incomes in post-divorce households irrespective of past behaviour. Seen in the light of Professor Barry's analysis, Lord Mackay's proposals seem bound to reduce people's incentives to get married, stay married, and behave properly within the marriage. This is not what most women want and it is not what is best for children.

Dr Glenn Wilson focuses upon the impact of biological sex differences on the positions of men and women at work. He claims that gender-equality cannot be achieved in all occupations. This is because average men and average women have different personalities, talents, and interests rooted in biological differences between them. For example, men tend to excel in mathematics and science and to be more competitive and motivated than women. Superior language skills and a greater interest in interpersonal relationships are characteristic of women. According to Dr Wilson, these sex differences cannot be accounted for by social forces. They result from differences in brain structure laid down under the influence of hormones during prenatal development. The sex differences which Wilson highlights may appear very small between average men and women, but they are important in determining excellence which is associated with career success.

Discrimination is unlikely to account for the fact that men rather than women tend to occupy the top positions in any work hierarchy. Dominance is a vital personality characteristic for getting to the top and it is determined by the presence of male hormones. Consequently, Dr Wilson finds it hard to support the feminist charge that women are under-represented at the top. It follows, therefore, that the widely-held belief in the glass-ceiling explanation of women's under-representation in top jobs is seriously misguided.

Achieving the feminist goals in relation to work is dependent upon getting the state to subsidise the costs of caring for the children of the ever-increasing numbers of mothers who go out to work. If state subsidies for childcare are not forthcoming, then the average women will not be able to afford to work full-time. If she does not work full-time, then she is unlikely to be able to compete with men, and the most efficient use of her time will, therefore, be looking after her own children. As unfair as that seems for feminists, most ordinary women automatically assume that they, together with their children's father, are responsible for caring for their own offspring. Of course, they are right but this sort of thinking is not compatible with the aims of feminism.

Professor Michael Levin discusses the childcare strategy currently being pursued by 'children's advocates' in the US. American society, according to Levin, is currently in the process of being deceived by feminists into supporting the break-up of the two-parent family and the socialisation of parenting. Feminists have for many years been pursuing an agenda which would result in the state paying for the upkeep of children, removing the necessity for women to marry in order to have children, and freeing them when they do from any childcare responsibilities. The costs of this strategy fall inevitably on society at large which includes responsible mothers and fathers who have resisted paying for other people's children when it is all they can do to provide for their own. By using child-friendly vocabulary and expressing concerns about 'our' children, however, feminists in the US are achieving more success in pursuing the same old goals.

Levin claims that Americans are being blackmailed by so-called children's advocates who promise to lift unmerited guilt about the deprived babies of irresponsible mothers and absent fathers if parenthood is socialised. The blackmail turns into extortion with warnings that today's under-privileged child is tomorrow's criminal. For Levin, special state provision for neglected children and their usually unmarried mothers signals that there is no need to worry about the consequences of having babies without the resources to support them.

Single parenthood, mass employment of mothers of young children, the reduction of time spent with children by their mothers, and marital instability are all, according to Professor Levin, social changes which, if not actually caused then, at least, are endorsed by feminism. The consequences of these changes include crime, deprivation, and poverty. He urges social scientists to brave the wrath of the feminists and make the results of their research known and help destroy the myth that feminism is on the side of virtue.

The final author, Joan Kennedy Taylor, is a self-identified feminist. Her central concern is not whether feminists' wants are desirable, for she assumes that they are. Rather, she asks why so many women are reluctant to admit that they are feminists. She explains that it is because feminism has challenged many of people's wishes which often are to fulfil traditional sex roles. These wishes, she argues in direct contrast to earlier authors, are not necessarily innate but have been formed against a background of tradition. It is, therefore, not surprising that the changes brought about by feminism are only appreciated in retrospect.

Taylor reviews the impact of feminism on women's lives and concludes that, on balance, it has been beneficial. She identifies two focuses within the feminist tradition: individualist feminism which is concerned with individual equality before the law, and relational feminism which is more concerned with achieving parity for women as a group and group rights. According to Taylor, it is the rise of a concern with group rights and the abandonment of individualist feminist ideals which may have brought feminism into disrepute. This is because group-rights feminism can easily result in individuals not being treated fairly in an effort to meet sex targets at work, for example. Taylor suggests combining the two strands in a way which would be more appealing to the average women. Equality before the law and individual rights should be feminist concerns in the public sphere and gender differences of concern in the private.

These essays have a number of striking policy implications. These include, first, amendment of equal opportunities legislation to permit employers once again to pay a family wage to the main bread-winner. Second, rejection of the Lord Chancellor's proposal to introduce no-fault divorce and, in its place, to revive the notion of marriage as based on a commitment for which the partners can and should be held to account. A third policy implication is that it is folly to seek to equalise the participation rates of the sexes in all spheres of employment, since there are perfectly sound reasons why there should be such differences between the sexes. Last but not least, there are important policy implications for the family. Since there are clear advantages in children being raised within the traditional two-parent family, then the state should pursue policies which actively support this institution rather than ones which undermine it.

6

What differentiates feminists on both right and left from non-feminists is the belief that the differences between the sexes are largely social artifacts and that, therefore, it is possible to equalise the status and roles of the two sexes. If, as they have been, governments are persuaded to promote the feminist agenda which assumes there to be no significant sex-differences (other than those most immediately associated with reproduction), and if the feminist view of the basis of sex-differences is mistaken (not a very big 'if' in view of the findings documented by Glenn Wilson), then what is designed to liberate women will only result in the oppression of men, women, and children alike. Adults of both sexes will be prevented from doing what comes naturally to them, and children deprived of the parental care and attention that is their due. The authors in the present collection make it imperative for all those concerned for women's well-being (not to mention the welfare of men and children) to reconsider the desirability of feminist prescriptions. Arguably, what women stand in most need of liberation from today is neither male oppression nor patriarchy, but the intellectual tyranny which so much modern feminism has become.

Feminism was not always so. As Joan Kennedy Taylor has recently observed, 'originally, in the early nineteenth century, the Woman Movement was a classical liberal, individualist movement'.[4] Even when, in the nineteen sixties, this movement underwent a dramatic revival, it still retained for a considerable time much of its original individualist character. It has only been in its most recent guise that feminism has acquired those totalitarian and collectivist features which the authors in this collection criticise.

The present collection of essays, therefore, is not anti-feminist in intent, if 'feminism' is taken to mean simply that movement which seeks to advance the interests and welfare of women. All they establish is that few of those marching today under the banner of feminism can be considered true friends of women or to speak on their behalf.

Two different forms of feminism, therefore, need to be clearly distinguished, one classical, the other modern. The former is feminism's original form, classical liberal in both inspiration and aspiration. The latter is a more recent and far more insidious

7

movement. Unfortunately, of late it is this latter form of feminism which has captured the head-lines and made the running in setting the policy agenda. Arguably, since women now enjoy the same civil and political rights as men, there is no longer any need today for a distinctly feminist perspective. Modern feminism is something from which today's women need liberation, if both sexes are fully to enjoy their common humanity.

Notes

1   Faludi, S., *Backlash: The Undeclared War Against Women*, London: Chatto & Windus, 1992.

2   Levin, M., *Feminism and Freedom*, New Brunswick, NJ: Transaction Books, 1987.

3   Wolf, N., *Fire with Fire: The New Female Power and How It Will Change the 21st Century*, London: Chatto & Windus, 1993.

4   Taylor, J.K., *Reclaiming the Mainstream: Individualist Feminism Rediscovered*, Buffalo, NY: Prometheus Books, 1992, p. 15.

Double Income, No Kids: The Case for a Family Wage

Patricia Morgan

Shirley is faced with a seemingly intractable problem:

> ... pretty and full of smiles, but her voice trembles when she mentions children. She keeps laughing as if what she is saying must be a bad joke. 'The big thing is that a lot of people moved here [Luton] about that time and now it is three or four years on and they all want families.' She laughs again. 'But the women can't afford to give up work because of the mortgage repayments.'
>
> 'I want a baby too', she says. 'I'm 35 years-old. But I can't, because of the situation. I might miss out on having a family altogether soon.' She says she feels as if she has an illness for which there is no cure.

The Independent, 2 June 1993.

Her sickness is endemic on both sides of the Atlantic—where the birth rate for dual earner couples is even lower than that of the overall population. Much of it is the effect of a living standard which has become based on a two, rather than a one, income norm.

It is the result of the mass entry of women into the workforce on the same terms as men, as the labour market has become 'feminised' and oriented towards female, rather than male, employment. Through tax and employment policies, government, under pressure from feminists, has exacerbated, rather than mitigated, the adverse effects on the ability of couples to found and maintain families.

The anti-family establishment urges more steps that will make a Shirley out of every prospective mother, with its pursuit of equal, or superior, outcomes for women in pay and position with men at all levels at all times. Instead of any proper understanding of the reasons for the old 'family wage' economy and the mechanisms which once made it possible to have

9

children and rear them at home on one income this is now anathematised as one of the great oppressions of history. Of course, the old ways involved limitations on female employment. But if women have exchanged these limitations for restrictions on their capacity to have and care for their own children, it is institutionalised feminism which has a vested interest in making sure that family and economy are at war, and women are unable to achieve a new compromise, reconciliation or balance between employment and parenthood.

Women in the Labour Force in the 1960s

In the first half of the twentieth century, women's workforce participation was concentrated in the years before marriage. Then, as Pearl Jephcott and others spelt out at the time,[1] the increase in married women working was happening for three major reasons: the extension of the lifespan not involved in childrearing, more jobs, and fewer single women to fill them. In 1850, the average woman had her first child at 28; her last child was five when she was 41.5 and her life expectancy was 46.5. A century later, the figures were 24.5, 31.25, and 72.5. The postwar pattern of high marriage rates and earlier marriage, had superimposed a reduced supply of women on top of a generally lower labour supply due to the low birth rates of the 1930s, and at a time of enhanced demand for labour. However, women were not competing for old established male jobs in industry and manufacture. They were going into the expanding private and public bureaucracies, service sectors, health, social and educational provisions.

Wives over 45 accounted for the ageing of the female labour force, as women either returned to work after their children were independent or worked part time with older children at home—using 'spare time' not involved in family responsibilities to add to the family's resources. The proportion of married women working was rising at the same time as the birth rate was high, for those joining the labour force were a different generation from the ones having children. Only nine per cent of women who had their first baby in 1945-47 returned to *any* paid work within six months of the birth and it took 30 years for the proportion to reach 17 per cent. In spite of an apparent transformation taking place in married women's work patterns, the increase in their 'extramural' activities was a corollary of the reduction, not rejection, of domestic responsibilities and these were subordinated and supplementary to their roles as wives and mothers. In 1964, the American president could still report to the United Nations that the wage system rested upon the principle of one main earner per family.

Starting a Better Home: Couples in the Workforce

But another movement was under way—if 38 per cent of British women who had their first child in 1940-44 did not work between marriage and the first birth, this had shrunk to 12 per cent by the 1970s. More important than the appearance of efficient contraception, was its promotion as a means to postpone as well as limit families. A gap between marriage and first birth not only promised to put women's growing training and education to use, and enable couples to enjoy their life together before babies came, it seemed to offer a chance of having a better living standard faster than the couple might have on the basis of the man's wage alone.

However, instead of being able to start a family with a higher living standard, a process began where both goals receded. A dedicated two-income strategy became increasingly necessary to maintain any living standard as prices rose to absorb two salaries.

Thus the decrease in the gap between the birth of the last child and the return to a job. By 1982, 80 per cent of childless couples under 30 had two earners, and the prospect of the loss of a goodly portion of their income just at the point where there are more to support. A family with two young children needs 57 per cent more than a childless couple to maintain the same living standard. The awesome demands on the man as 'sole supporter' are illustrated by the way that (at 1992 prices), two adults and two young children need a minimum of £345.88 a week (as established owner occupiers, outside London), compared to £265.31 for a bachelor (or only £150.34 if he is a tenant).[2]

Equal Earner: Two Earners

Equal pay and the elimination of gender differentiation from the labour market has pushed incentives in the direction of the two-income household. At first, the 'rights movement' wanted equal opportunities for the equally qualified, but this soon changed to equal outcomes, and the dismantling of barriers turned to positive recruitment to ensure that women are not 'under represented' anywhere.

The rise in women's net earnings in relation to men has been a major contributor to the way in which births have been insufficient to replace the population since the mid 1970s.[3] The two-income norm resting on sex equality in the workplace makes childrearing an expensive use of women's time in terms of the returns foregone from virtually any paid occupation. The higher her earnings at marriage, the older she is at the time of the first birth and the smaller her family. Where married women earn as much as or more than their husbands, the pressure is never to give up work, however briefly. Over 80 per cent of middle and upper management women in top companies surveyed in 1990 had no children even if, like Shirley, they gave love and family a higher priority than career success.[4]

A Feminised Workforce

The entry of women into the workforce on the same, or even better, terms as men, has been accompanied not just by the continuing growth in jobs suited to women, but the wholesale clearance of more highly paid 'men's jobs' in the old unionised, heavy, extractive and manufacturing industries. At the very visible level of managerial and professional employment, young women might be rising more rapidly and out-earning their male counterparts. However, apart from an upward spurt in women's wage rates after equal pay legislation, the dwindling overall male–female gap increasingly represents stagnating or declining male wages. Thus, while the proportion of full-time British women paid below the Council of Europe's 'decency threshold'—set at 68 per cent of full-time mean earnings—fell from 57.6 per cent to 50.7 per cent between 1979 and 1992, the male proportion climbed from 14.6 per cent to 28.7 per cent.[5]

But while women's contribution to the growth of the workforce has been loudly acclaimed as men's participation has fallen, quieter voices suggest that the rise of women workers helped companies to see the benefit of temporary and part-time work and to restructure jobs so that they can be filled by contingent, cheaper workers. Part-time employment can account for all the jobs created over the last decade as well as the growth in women in paid work since the 1970s who, in turn, account for the growth in the workforce. As living expenses emphasize how impractical it is to forego the wife's contribution, the same processes that leave men unable to support a family alone draw into the labour market women who are anxious to boost family income or who, as lone mothers, are able to get their wages made up out of public assistance—where the flow accelerates even if female earning power does not.[6]

So what began as moves by women amidst greater opportunities to add to their occupational satisfaction, or to utilise time not taken up caring for the family to increase its comforts, now reflects the family's mounting insecurity and impoverishment, as paid work competes with prime childrearing time.

Maternal Resistance

The structure of their employment also reflects the resistance of mothers to paid work. Only three per cent of the population are in favour of both parents working full time: 76 per cent want the mothers of under five year-olds completely at home and 93 per cent want the fathers working full time.[7] The proportion of married mothers in full-time work may have doubled over the decade, but only to 11 per cent in 1990, compared to 27 per cent in part-time work—(for under tens the figures are 17 per cent and 48 per cent and for under fifteens, they are 27 per cent and 45 per cent). Moreover, fully employed mothers are far more dissatisfied with their lot than those working part time or not at all—even when jobs are those like nurse, manager, lawyer and laboratory technician.[8] If a recent Gallup survey of working mothers of infants found that 62 per cent would be at home if money was not a problem (and 82 per cent in the low income bracket), it replicates other studies where two-thirds or more of British or American dual-income families want a parent at home.[9]

Preference for their own care is another reason why women who would have to remain in full-time work if they had children tend to postpone or forego births, or limit these to one.

The growth of women in better paid, high status employment over time is largely a function of the absence of dependent children—throughout, or at both ends of the working life. Otherwise, mothers tend to keep their working hours to a minimum necessary to meet basic commitments. There is the downward trend in hours worked as the number of part-time workers swells. In 1979, 29.8 per cent of female manual part-time workers (and 23 per cent of non-manual) worked less than 16 hours a week. By 1990, the figures were 43.7 per cent and 31.8 per cent as the proportion working less than eight hours also rose.[10]

Such developments are reminiscent of the effects of Sweden's model 'equality program'. In the 1970s Sweden's tax and labour market policies made the one-earner family unviable; it soon led the Western world with about 85 per cent of mothers of children under seven years at work. But it also achieved the highest proportion of women working part time or only nominally in work at all (being registered unemployed or sick). As mothers took irregular, low-paid jobs, the average hours worked by all women dropped and, if industrial wage rates for women reached 90 per cent of men's, women's actual earnings only averaged 50 per cent to 65 per cent of men's. Even given childcare, few mothers wanted responsible jobs with children in crèches for ten or more hours a day.[11]

Putting on the Tax Squeeze

Britain's anti-family trends in taxation have meant that, as the tax burden has moved downwards since the 1960s, those with dependent children have been the hardest hit. At the same time, the system bears hardest on one-earner couples. The income tax threshold alone fell from 101.2 per cent to 36.3 per cent of average male manual earnings for a married man with two small children between 1950 and 1992—and owes much to the demise of child tax allowances. If we also take family allowances (child benefit) into account, the break-even point at which a married man with two children paid no net tax was 124.5 per cent in 1950, but 64.6 per cent in 1992 (or 188.2 per cent compared to 87.4 per cent for four children).[12]

The tax threshold for a one-earner family is lower than for the combined income of a couple where both are employed—or

£5,165 and £7,597 in 1992-3—and they can earn twice £23,700 before being liable to pay the higher, or 40 per cent rate of tax. A couple with one income of £40,000 gross had £27,984 after tax and national insurance in 1992-3, while a two income couple earning £25,000 and £15,000 had £29,495 (paying £7,597 income tax compared to £10,254). The higher tax bill means that a couple with two children needed a wage of £21,156 in 1992 for a modest budget, compared with £19,401 for two earners.

Traditionally, a married couple had 2.5 times the single or personal tax allowance when both are in paid work and 1.5 where there is one earner (the marriage allowance being half of the personal tax allowance). In 1986, a Green Paper proposed removing discrimination against families with one main earner and reducing their tax burden by giving everyone a basic tax allowance which one spouse could transfer to the other if they themselves did not earn enough to set against it. Condemning this as a disincentive for mothers to work, establishment feminists played a major role in its defeat. They have also campaigned tirelessly for the removal of the Married Couple's Allowance (MCA), which was Labour Party policy by the 1980s, and is now being implemented by John Major's Tory administration. The Government's feminist advisors have offered this up to pay off the public sector borrowing requirement, and to create lower tax bands—which disproportionately benefit double earners and the single and childless, as the tax burden on those with dependents increases with the removal of their allowances.

The MCA may go to childless couples, but also every working family (and employed lone parents). After the removal of the child tax allowance, it has been the only recognition of the extra costs of those with family responsibilities left in the tax system. Abolition puts the one-income family in the same income tax position as a single, childless person as, at the same time, they are paying 25 per cent more than a bachelor in local taxation. It also makes the one-income family's position even more asymmetrical compared to couples with two full incomes (making the allowance ratio one to two). If the MCA had not been frozen at its 1990-91 level of £1,720, it would be worth £2,400 in 1993-4. The Treasury has already made £1,750 million and stands to make a further £900 million in 1994-5 by giving relief only at the lowest or 20 per cent tax rate, rather than at the main 25 per cent or 40 per cent levels.

As intended, this halving of the value of the remaining MCA will have its most damaging impact in the crucial income band between £20,000 and £30,000. Here it might be possible for one earner to sustain a family, given that the MCA provided some relief from the imposition of higher rate tax on solo family incomes in this range. Instead, husbands lose £344 on top of the £168 resulting from freezing.[13]

This treatment is justified on the grounds that men no longer support families—where the rise in the number of working wives is used to suggest that all *mothers* are fully employed and entirely 'self-sufficient'. Yet, fathers provide 87.8 per cent of household income where they are the sole family earner and 69 per cent where the mother is employed (4 out of 5 part-time women contribute less than 30 per cent of household income).

Make Them Poor and Force Them Out

In fact, what really exercises the equality activist is that, although each age group of women is spending more time at work:

> A typical woman in the UK having 2 children ... has 9 years less full-time employment than a woman who has no children, but 2.8 years more part-time employment—producing a net loss of 6 years paid work.
>
> ... more than 80 per cent of women leave the labour market for a period after the birth of their first child, and only 3 per cent remain in the labour market throughout their childbearing years.[14]

In turn, since the earnings of most mothers are 'not sufficient to provide economic independence', the 'cost' of caring for children is 'financial dependence ... on a spouse'.[15] Thus the family has an iniquitous role in maintaining inequality—both as an obstacle to the full representation of women everywhere to the same or greater degree than men, and to women acquiring incomes sufficient to enable them and their children to escape all economic dependence on men.

Of course, it is clear that, whatever is still intoned about employer discrimination to explain the average wage of women (at 79.1 per cent of men's), the remaining gap is not explainable in terms of opportunities denied. Young single women earn almost as much as single men. By their mid thirties, they begin to earn more—as men who stay unmarried reduce their efforts.[16] What happens is that married men increase, and young married women decrease, their work efforts. But if over 90 per cent of mothers still insist that their family is more important than other domains of life and most, whether employed or not, do not consider paid work more fulfilling than parenthood,[17] the equality activist turns their choices into key components of the conspiracy against them. If motherhood is 'the lynchpin' of the family's 'excruciating' oppressiveness, cutting women off from self-realisation,[18] so 'dominant ideologies around motherhood and the male breadwinning role' prevent them from understanding how much they are oppressed.[19]

Wives see their husbands' jobs as a basis for 'material and financial security and "a good family life"'.[20] But to the equality activist, the way in which male 'earnings are largely unaffected by fatherhood and can be enhanced by marriage',[21] is *prima facie* evidence that men use the family as a resource to exploit for their economic self-interest and their wage to keep their wives in bondage. If hours at work are longest where there are dependent children and as the family's economic position worsened in the 1980s, men take second jobs, overtime and shifts, it is to reinforce the 'gender division of labour' and consolidate their advantage when women are incapacitated by childcare.[22]

What makes equality activists livid is the way that many couples approach parenthood by trying to manage on one income—saving or otherwise putting the wife's income aside for extras or emergencies. This is actually a shrewd survival strategy, aimed at increasing the family's economic resilience and room to manoeuvre. But if those involved see themselves as clearing a way, rather than erecting barriers, to procreation, the activist sees only the 'marginalising' of women in the marketplace.

Same Income: Double Workload

When couples effectively stand on or near the same economic position with two incomes as they might previously have occupied on one, the duplication of effort denies them access to the division of labour—which otherwise enables them to cover all aspects of the parental role. And children must have third-party care—but where is this?

Despite the widespread assumption that childrearing costs somehow vanish once these are no longer experienced by the mother in terms of wages foregone, mothers find that the price of substitute care may take much or all of what they earn. This is then seen to necessitate the manifest absurdity of 'comprehensive' childcare provisions—that are 'high quality', so not as to damage children, and 'affordable', or cheaper than the mother's labour. Yet, nurseries are an almost unimaginably expensive and difficult way of looking after children. To provide care at any reasonable standard, requires one qualified carer to three infants, plus the places and personnel to train them and well equipped centres with stable groups of preferably no more than 10 small children.[23] Having depleted the family's resources, the state is meant to take on the children that parents cannot afford to look after—by providing institutions at a cost well beyond that of any allowance that would permit them to be better reared at home.

Pricing Out Parenting

A two-income norm makes it difficult for couples to co-operate effectively. Even if fathers—who are likely to be working longer hours—increase their share of household tasks, each parent must put in more hours to meet basic demands. The price for two full-time workers is immense in terms of constant fatigue, pressure and overload—where, 'in no other situation was so much conflict so consistently reported'.[24] Fathers experience more stress than childless men; but if dual-earner fathers are most stressed of all,[25] then neither parent provides the other with the buffering which may have been available when only men developed market skills in the childrearing years. If balancing job and family demands is often extremely difficult for parents with older children, they are most incompatible in the early years.

Parents who have low occupational status and take the child to non-home based care, or operate shifts, where the mother leaves for work when the father comes home, are also more stressed than the highly publicised women with interesting, high paid careers, who can afford help at home. Parents not only have fewer children, but spend less time with the one(s) they have, and less time together as a family in which to maintain common perspectives. Added to family breakdown and the desertion of fathers, the increase in working hours and the shift of mothers into the workforce means declining parental attention, and a fall in the general 'contact' time that adults have with children.[26]

Children placed first in their parents' allocation of time and attention show superior skills. Therefore, when economic pressures make homemaking a 'wasteful' use of time, we may expect a reduction in the quality of the child 'product' as maternal labour is put to more 'profitable' use. Early resumption of employment is expressly associated with low investment in parenthood, which affects the security of attachments and generally lowers the quality of parenting.[27] The trade-off between full-time maternal employment and child development is seen in its negative relationship with educational stimulation at home, academic achievement and behaviour recorded at various ages, regardless of socio-economic status.[28]

History Repeats Itself

We have been here before. It was Frederick Engels who described how, in the 1840s:

> ... the employment of the wife dissolves the family utterly and of necessity, and this dissolution, in our present society, which is based upon the family, brings the most demoralising consequences for parents as well as children. A mother who has no time to trouble herself about her child, to perform the most ordinary and loving services for it during its first year, must inevitably grow indifferent to it, treat it unlovingly like a stranger. The children who grow up under such conditions are utterly ruined for later family life, can never feel at home in the family which they themselves found, because they have always been accustomed to isolation, and they contribute to the already general undermining of the family in the working class.[29]

One response to the way in which early industrialisation broke the mechanisms which sustained a 'family wage' in the old world of guilds and companies was, as today, for the family to push more labour onto the market in an attempt to meet costs. However by vastly expanding the supply of labour, the capitalisation of women's and children's earnings militated against longer-term improvement. As this undercut the wages, or destroyed the livelihoods of able-bodied men, the family man had to accept children's work at children's wages. The family gained little in exchange for the sacrifice of its nurturing and socialising functions: its resources even declined as wages were driven down.

A Great Calamity of History?

In consequence, the early labour movement came to press for the establishment of a 'living wage', one sufficient for a man to support his wife and children at a modest level of comfort. In turn, the 'measure of a decent wage' was, as a 'pro-labor American newspaper editorialised in the 1880s ... one sufficient for a man "to keep his wife and children out of competition with himself"'.[30] Campaigns to end child labour and revaluations of married women's work were instrumental to this end. Jobs might be more vigorously sorted into male and female categories, with many of the 'female' ones considered of short duration—until marriage, or as an alternative. Protective legislation progressively restricted the hours or nature of women's work (usually dated from the 1842 Mines Act). Wage differentials also solidified, with the higher wages of men invariably justified on the grounds that a man had an actual or prospective wife and children to support.

Today, this is usually represented as a process in which women were silenced and herded into the home and the very worst aspect of the protection built around the family in the past—all of which is now seen to bear witness to maleficent purposes.[31] Feminists often define the awful 'patriarchal' family as one in which 'the husband is employed ... in the workplace and the wife is not employed outside the home'.[32] It is said to have its origins in the moves of patriarchy (or maybe patriarchy in collusion with capitalism) to re-oppress women and children after they had been temporarily liberated by early industrialisation.[33]

View From The Women

However, a wealth of historical data shows how women were involved in a quite conscious development and clarification of

20

their relationships to work, home and fellow employees.[34] They found the idea of one wage for one breadwinner highly desirable and—overwhelmingly agreeing that this breadwinner must be the man—they willingly endorsed restrictions on female labour to get it. Women saw employment as something prior to marriage or childbearing after which they moved in and out of work according to family need. Here they wished to increase the security and protection of their work and improve conditions for all employees, while fighting for alternatives which would remove them from the factory altogether. Typically:

> In the midst of the Preston lockout Margaret Fletcher, the leading woman orator, lamented what she considered a reversal of the natural order of things, which forced a woman to leave home and family at 5.30 a.m. and go to work while her husband stayed at home. Men must have a fair day's pay for a fair day's work ... which would enable them to maintain themselves and their families in comfort while their wives remained at home to take care of the house and educate the children. During the strikes among the power-loom weavers in 1878, women played an active part ... Yet ... also raised the demand for the withdrawal of married women from the factory.[35]

It is often argued that none of this needed to be, if the jobs market had been one of equal opportunity in the first place (so that women would not have crowded into lowly work which then cried out for protective legislation). But even if equality was achievable other than in the abstract, the result—of both spouses working to support the home—was just not attractive.

Prior to the 1960s, it is difficult to find a brand of feminism that expressly downgraded childrearing, opposed the family or the roles of men and women in it. Feminists tended to be leading advocates of measures to foster the special contribution of mothers. Their demands for political rights and reform of the marriage laws accompanied moves to enhance the status of women in the home. They wanted women to enjoy a choice between the professions and public office or remaining at home and agreed that, if mothers supported families financially, this would be a further and unfair burden on women, which detracted from the care of children.

They also realised that women's occupational advance and the protection of the family economy were not necessarily opposed. Indeed, career women often saw married female labour as just as much a threat to their ability to earn a reasonable living for themselves, as it was to men's. Hence they willingly supported moves to forestall competition from hard pressed secondary earners. When Eleanor Rathbone, in her much misread *Disinherited Family* of 1924, argued for equal pay and an end to gender restrictions in employment, she also insisted that families must be compensated for the loss of the man's 'living wage' through the vigorous development of occupational and/or state child and homemaking allowances. She warned against attempts to achieve parity in outcome for men and women which made it impossible for families to live on one wage.

Worthless Bondage

It is arguable whether the movement of women (and children) out of employment was among the causes or effects of the rising real wages (estimated as in the region of 55 per cent to 79 per cent) of men between 1850 and 1910—as the number of married women in some paid employment dropped from over a half to around 10 per cent.[36] An interactive process is likely, which continued through to the 1960s. A wage sufficient to provide for basic needs was necessary if the household was to be supported by one earner—and this might only be possible if women left the labour force in large numbers. In turn, rising wages led to an increased demand for domestic labour and gave married women the opportunity to invest in homemaking.

Modern historians like to see housewives, past and present, as engaged in utterly demeaning, monotonous and meaningless work that brings no financial remuneration and produces nothing of intrinsic value. But, while there are advantages and disadvantages in both domestic work and waged labour, paid employment can double the workload without necessarily increasing what is produced. As Joanna Bourke[37] reminds us, meals do not spring out of the table—they have to be planned, bought, cooked and presented. In other words, living standards have to be created out of money. When economists talk of the increased prosperity of working-class households as we enter the twentieth century, what is easy to overlook is that such consumption cannot occur without an investment of labour, to manage income and convert this into consumable goods. Domestic work also improves the productivity of present and future wage earners by improved health and nutrition.

Ensuring the Value of Homemaking

The immediate effect on family economics where there is a clear difference between the earnings of men and women, is that couples are 'better off' than if they operate alone, since it enables them to exploit a division of labour. With a higher earning capacity, the husband gives his time to paid employment, and this makes housework 'cheaper' when supplied by his wife. In turn, increases in the husband's earnings raise the value of the wife's time at home. A division of labour enables each party to specialise, making their joint output larger than the sum of what they produce singly—and the gains will be more the bigger the differences in the wage rate that each can command.[38] If the man can earn more than his wife, then it is more advantageous for the family if he increases his work where the family needs extra income.

Since childbearing and most childrearing is done by women then, as stated, when higher real wages mean higher women's wages, the impetus for married women to work outweighs the disincentive for them not to work even where their husbands may be well off. This does not mean that a couple can afford more children, for women's increased earning potential also increases what is perceived as the cost in terms of earnings foregone. But higher men's wages impose no such costs. Representing an overall gain for the family, this makes children more 'affordable'.

Not too long ago, means were found to relieve both the direct costs of childrearing—and thus the contrast between a living standard without children and relative poverty with them—and the opportunity costs. Now we are invited to read these costs for an adverse judgement on childrearing and an unproductive use of the mother's time. If Heather Joshi keeps telling us how much children cost mothers,[39] she does not recognise how fathers might, even now, make up some of these lost earnings. But then, any notion of commitment to the joint resources of a family is missing from a perspective which recognises only 'independent incomes for women' in terms of personal spending money which, curiously, is not even meant to carry the costs of substitute childcare. Her answer—to push more women into the workforce so none can afford to stay out—drives up the very opportunity costs which are used to decry maternal care.

Policies for Parenthood

For the Shirleys of this world to be able to have and care for their children, there must be greater respect for the priorities of couples themselves as to how they allocate their labour over their lifetime. And it may have to be accepted that men will predominate in the labour force in the childrearing years, after which women will be more prominent—when men's wages fall as women's rise.

But all the paternal effort in the world will not keep a family if it is taxed away. More, not less, consideration must be given to the precarious position of families coping with an equal wage economy. Allowing tax allowances to be fully transferable within families (from spouse to spouse and from child to parent) should remove the low and middle-income earner from tax liability where either is the main, or only, provider.

At present, not only is social security expenditure dominated by the growing bill for state pensions, but a vast and fast increasing amount of tax relief is available to provide for decades of affluent leisure when there are no dependent children, while families are suffering a worsening deficit of time and resources for investment in the future productivity of the nation. Societies can function without retirement—indeed, mass provision of substantial labour-free incomes for adults will break the back of any economy—but not without families equipped to maintain the next generation. There is not only a need to reverse the growing trend to earlier retirement, but to reschedule payments for pension plans to the latter half of the working life—and divert some of the massive government subsidies into insurance schemes for parenthood. The narrow focus on child benefit provided through the benefits system detracts from the possibility of personal and occupational family allowance schemes. Whether run by employers, professional associations, friendly societies or trade unions, such 'wage equalisation funds' were once widespread here and abroad, as a way of spreading the extra costs of parents and providing for overloaded points in the life cycle.

Childcare vouchers, subsidies for workplace nurseries and childcare tax relief are the nearest we have come to reinventing these schemes when what is needed is help for parents, male and female, that allows them to choose whether they spend family allowances on their own care or that of substitutes.

Notes

1 Jephcott, P., Seear, N. and Smith, J.H., *Married Women Working*, London: George Allen & Unwin, 1962; see also Negler, C.N., *At Odds: Women and the Family in America*, Oxford University Press, 1980.

2 'Household Budgets and Living Standards', *Social Policy Research Findings* No. 31, Rowntree Foundation, November 1992.

3 Schultz, T.P., 'Testing the Neoclassical Model of Family Labor Supply and Fertility', *The Journal of Human Resources*, XXV, 4, 1991, pp. 599-624. Ermisch, J., 'Economic Influences on Birthrates', *National Economic Review*, November 1988; Ermisch, J., *Fewer Babies, Longer Lives*, Joseph Rowntree Foundation, 1990.

4 Commissioned by Guardian Royal Exchange, Report in *Daily Mail*, 14 November 1990.

5 Low Pay Unit estimates based on *New Earnings Survey*, Table A24.1, 1993.

6 Carlson, A.C., 'What Happened to the 'Family Wage'?', *The Public Interest*, pp. 3-17, 1986.

7 Ashford, S., 'Family Matters', in Jowell, R., *et al.*, (eds.), *British Social Attitudes*, Aldershot: Gower, 1988.

8 Tresch Owen, M. and Cox, M.J., 'The Transition to Parenthood', in Gottfried, A.E., Gottfried, A.W. and Bathurst, K., *Maternal Employment, Family Environment and Children's Development*, Plenum Press, 1988.

9 The 1992 Farley Report.

10 Low Pay Unit, *The New Review* No. 8, 1991; Luckhaus, L. and Dickens, *Social Protection of Atypical Workers in the United Kingdom*, Brussels: European Commission, 1991; and Marsh, C., 'Hours of Work of Women and Men in Britain', *EOC Research Series*, London: HMSO, 1991.

11 Lewis, H., *Sweden's Right to be Human*, Allison and Busby Ltd., 1982; also Broberg, A. and Hwang, C.P., 'Day Care for Young Children in Sweden', in Melhuish, E.C. and Moss, P., (eds.), *Day Care for Young Children: International Perspectives*, Tavistock/Routledge, 1991; and Morgan, P., *Families in Dreamland*, London: Social Affairs Unit, 1992.

12 Inland Revenue Statistics 1993, *The Reforms Of Personal Taxation*, London: HMSO, 1986.

13 Relief will be reduced to 15 per cent from 1995, causing even larger losses.

14 Moss, P., 'Childcare and Equality of Opportunity: Consolidated Report to the European Commission', Brussels: EOC, April 1988, p. 21.

15 Lister, R., *Women's Economic Dependency and Social Security*, Research Discussion Series No. 2, EOC, 1992, p. 16; and Glendinning, C., 'Dependency and Interdependency: the Incomes of Informal Carers and the Impact of Social Security', *Journal of Social Policy*, Vol. 19, 4, 1990, pp. 469-97.

16 Levin, M., *Feminism and Freedom*, New Brunswick, NJ: Transaction Books, 1987.

17 Moss, P., Bollard, G. and Foxman, R., 'Transition to Parenthood: A Report to the DHSS', Mimeographed report, Thomas Coram Research Unit, London University, 1983; Mansfield, P. and Collard, J., *The Beginning of the Rest of Your Life*, London: MacMillan, 1988.

18 Niva, M., 'From Utopian to Scientific Feminism? Early Feminist Critiques of the Family', in Segal, L., *What's to be Done About the Family?*, Harmondsworth: Penguin, 1987.

19 Lister, R., *op. cit.*, p. 20.

20 Mansfield, P. and Collard, J., *op. cit.*, p. 141-42.

21 Cohen, B., *Caring for Children: Services and Policies for Childcare and Equal Opportunities in the United Kingdom*, Brussels: Commission of the European Communities, 1988, p. 15.

22 Moss, P. and Brannen, J., 'Fathers and Unemployment', in Lewis, C. and O'Brien, M., *Reassessing Fatherhood*, London: Sage, 1987, p. 42.

23 Phillips, D.A. and Howes, C., 'Indicators of Quality in Child Care: Review of the Research', in Phillips, D.A., (ed.), *Quality in Child Care: What Does Research Tell Us?*, Research Monograph of the National Association for the Education of Young Children, 1987; Belsky, J., 'Two Waves of Day Care Research: Developmental Effects and Conditions of Quality', in Ainslie, R., (ed.), *The Child and the Day Care Setting*, Praeger, 1984, pp. 1-34.

24 Daniels, P. and Weingarten, K., *Sooner or Later*, W.W. Norton & Co., 1982.

25 Goldberg, W.A. and Easterbrooks, M.A.,'Maternal Employment when Children are Toddlers and Kindergartners', in Gottfried, A.E. *et al., op. cit.*; Lewis, S.N.C. and Cooper, C.L., 'Stress in Two-Earner Couples and Stage in the Life Cycle', *Journal of Occupational Psychology*, 60, 1987, pp. 289-303.

26 See Matox Jr., W.R., 'So Many Bills, So Little Time', *Policy Review*, Winter, No. 55, 1991, pp. 8-10;

27 Hughes, D., and Galinsky, E., 'Balancing Work and Family Responsibilities', in Gottfried, A.E. *et al., op. cit.*

28 Baydar, N. and Brooks-Gunn, J., 'Effects of Maternal Employment and Child-Care Arrangements on Preschoolers' Cognitive and Behavioural Outcomes: Evidence from the Children of the National Longitudinal Survey of Youth', *Developmental Psychology*, Vol. 27, No. 6, 1991, pp.

932-45; Stafford, F.P., 'Women's Work, Sibling Competition, and Children's Performance', *The American Economic Review*, 77, 1987, pp. 972-80.

29 Engels, F., *The Condition of the Working Class in England*, Panther, 1979, first published 1892, p. 172.

30 Quoted in Carlson, A.C., 'What Happened To the 'Family Wage'?', *The Public Interest*, 1986, pp. 3-17.

31 For example: Lewis, J., *The Politics of Motherhood: Child and Maternal Welfare in England 1900-1939*, London: Croom Helm, 1980, p. 21.

32 Lopata, H.Z., 'The Interweave of Public and Private: Women's Challenge to American Society', *Journal of Marriage and the Family*, 55, 1993, pp. 176-90.

33 For example, Secombe, W., 'The Housewife and Her Labour Under Capitalism', *New Left Review*, No. 83, 1974, p. 19; also 'Patriarchy Stabilised: The Construction of the Male Breadwinner Wage Norm in Nineteenth Century Britain', *Social History*, xi, No. 1, 1986, pp. 53-76.

34 For example: Morgan, C.E., 'Women, Work and Consciousness in the Mid-Nineteenth Century English Cotton Industry', *Social History*, Vol. 17, No. 1, 1992, pp. 23-41.

35 *Ibid.*, pp. 40-41.

36 Bourke, J., 'How to be Happy Though Married: Housewifery in Working Class Britain 1860-1914', in press.

37 *Ibid.*

38 Becker, G.S., *A Treatise on the Family*, Harvard University Press, 1981.

39 Joshi, H., *The Cash Opportunity Cost of Childbearing in Britain*, CEPR Discussion Paper No. 157, 1987.

The Family:
A Matriarchal Institution

Mary Kenny

In the canon of contemporary feminism, the Family is usually seen as an oppressive, patriarchal institution maliciously designed to make women miserable. 'The family supports capitalism by providing a way for calm to be maintained amidst the disruption that is very much part of capitalism,' says *A Feminist Dictionary*:

> It supports capitalist economy by providing a productive labour force and supplying a market for massive consumption. In its convention-alised, white form ... [the family] provides a model of gender and generation hierarchies for the social relations of factories, schools, universities, business corporations, religious organisations, political parties, governments, armies and hospitals. An institution for the more complete subjugation and enslavement of women and children. Comes from the Latin *famulus*, meaning a servant or slave which is itself a reminder that wives and children, along with servants were historically part of a man's property.[1]

You get the picture. The family is a male chauvinist plot and the tragedy of it is that it seems to have been such a successful one. But not for much longer, perhaps? In Western societies now the traditional family is perceived to be everywhere in decline: certainly there is an explosion in divorce, in cohabita-tion and in the voluntary choice of single-parenthood, and what is most marked is that it *seems* that women are leading the way in these choices. Between 1981 and 1989, in Britain, the marriage rate began to fall noticeably, but it was women, more than men, who showed greater reluctance to go to the altar.[2] Women also show more willingness to divorce: the majority of divorce petitions are now sought by women. Women regret divorce less: it is claimed that while one-third of men regret dissolving their first marriages, only one-quarter of women do so.[3]

Divorce does have a deleterious effect on the health of individuals. Divorced individuals die sooner, are more likely to have headaches, chest pains, hypertension, alcohol problems, and even cancer; they are more inclined to suicide and accidents too.[4] But in all these cases the deterioration is more marked in men than in women. Women seem to be able to live without marriage more than men, as a general rule. As our grandmothers might have put it, men go to pieces if they do not have someone to look after them.

Our grandmothers, however, generally firmly believed in marriage for both their daughters and their sons, but, very likely, worried more about getting their daughters married than their sons. For it used to be said that 'all women should be married, but no man', and that courtship meant that 'a man pursues a woman until she catches him'. It was also held that 'marriage is the price that men pay for sex, and sex is the price that women pay for marriage'. How very Victorian! Today, the extreme views of radical women like Eleanor Marx, Emma Goldman and Alexandra Kollontai, who maintained that marriage was akin to prostitution, that it sold women into slavery and that it served only men and 'exploitative capitalism' are perfectly acceptable in mainstream bourgeois society, and millions of women act upon these theories. Conventional marriage and family life seems to be in irrevocable decline in an age which now rejects patriarchy.

Marriage: A Patriarchal Construct?

It is certainly true that Western marriage can be seen as a patriarchal construct, if we consider how carefully women were 'controlled' within marriage. Not until the Married Women's Property Act of 1882 could married women hold property in their own right. Until then, as men and women were 'one person in law', the 'very being or legal existence of the woman is suspended during the marriage, or at least incorporated or consolidated into that of her husband, under whose wing, protection and cover, she performs everything,' as one Victorian legal commentator explained.[5] Even the children of the marriage were 'held to be the property of the husband' and 'the mother might at any time be denied access to them'. Even after the Custody of Infants Act of 1886,—a predecessor to the Children

Act in that it was designed to take into consideration the best interest of the child—'the father remained during his lifetime their sole legal guardian'.

In theory, too, the woman's body legally belonged to her husband; if she left the house, right up until the 1890s, he could virtually take her prisoner and insist she return under a writ of *habeas corpus*. As her body was his, her house was generally his. Until recent times not only was a husband exempt from any charges of raping his wife, but invasive forms of contraception—the coil, for example—commonly required a husband's written permission.

These traditions were not exclusively English: the *Code Napoleon*, so admired in France as an example of codified law, restored to the father of the family the paternal power that had been, briefly, undermined by the upheaval of the Revolution, and established in law the dependency of the females upon the males of the family. Napoleon had firm ideas about a woman's place:

> Women in these days require restraint ... It is not French to give women the upper hand; they have too much of it already. There are more women who wrong their husbands than men who wrong their wives. We want a bridle for the class of women who commit adultery for gewgaws, for verses, Apollo and the muses, and all the rest of it.[6]

In fact, everywhere we look in the developed world we see that the traditional family *is* patriarchal: British, French, German, American, Mediterranean, Slav, Japanese, Jewish ... The more traditional the society, in many respects, the more patriarchal: Islam, India, China—societies which do not welcome girls as much as boys into the world, societies, indeed, where there are well-founded suspicions that infanticide or late abortions of girl babies are taking place, in consideration of the unnatural balance in the population of infant boys to girls. Less developed societies could scarcely be said to fare better either: Africa, Asia, Polynesia, Latin America. In many of these parts of the world women are unfortunate drudges, the slaves of slaves, the hewers of wood and the drawers of water, the beasts of burden.

Male chauvinism is a very widely dispersed phenomenon and a very deeply engrained tradition which may be impossible to erase. John Stuart Mill may have said that the 'only' problem with the subjugation of women is that it was merely 'custom-ary' rather than 'natural'. But custom and nature can sometimes be devilishly difficult to separate in a which-comes-first-the-chicken-or-the-egg enigma.

Healthy People: Single Women and Married Men

The notion that marriage and the family principally serviced men—though it had been present in Marxist ideas since the mid-nineteenth century—probably entered the mainstream of sociological thinking with the publication of Jessie Bernard's study *The Future of Marriage* in 1972.[7]

Dr Bernard, an American sociologist, demonstrated in this work—which mixed a very thorough attention to data with an accessible style, before the period when feminists (and sociologists) took to writing in impenetrable jargon—how women's health and mental well-being were diminished by marriage; whereas men's health and well-being were enhanced. Several studies since those, including those by Dr Jack Dominian of One Plus One,[8] the marriage research centre in London (which is ardently pro-marriage), have corroborated the Bernard findings. The healthiest people in the population, mentally and physically, tend to be single women and married men.

Marriage, it emerged in Jessie Bernard's study, was *paid for* by women's health and anxiety. In the light of the data that she had before her, Dr Bernard went on to speculate about the future of marriage, and how it could be organised (or if it was to be organised at all) so as to diminish this negative impact on women. The future of marriage had to be different from the past, anyhow, she explained, since so much of Christian (and, although she does not give other traditions much weight, the same is true in other cultures) traditions about marriage centre on the importance of virginity and fidelity: which, after the invention of the Pill, no longer seem as important. Pre-marriage sex was now accepted by the younger generation (in 1970, when she was writing): soon, extra-marital sex would seem just as acceptable. The notion of male control, which underpinned so much of marriage and family traditions, would, she hoped, with enlightenment, disappear. Future marriage, she insisted, would have to be based on equality, inside and outside the home, and on better arrangements for domestic life—such as the idea of

31

young couples in a community eating together in a communal cafeteria, rather than having to make their own inefficient, private arrangements at home, usually undertaken by the woman.

Bernard's sociology was impressive because it was based on a close, intelligent and energetic consideration of the data, organised in a way that brought fresh insight: it deserved its position (possibly more than some of the better-known feminist tracts of the time) as a milestone in feminist studies.

But few individuals can predict the future: extrapolating from present data into times to come is always flawed because circumstances alter. Extrapolating from present problems is rather like the London County Councillors who were so concerned in the 1890s with the accumulation of horse droppings in the West End, and fretted their brains as to how the problem would be solved thirty years hence. What they did not envisage was the disappearance altogether of horse-drawn vehicles with the proliferation of the motor car. Dr Bernard could not have predicted the oil crisis of 1973, the economic crises that followed, the rise of Reaganism-Thatcherism, the crash of Communism, and mass unemployment. Her notion of 'communal kitchens' is not only Maoist—at one stage, Mao arbitrarily banned eating at home in his drive to send families into communal kitchens—but 1930s-utopian. Concerned social reformers such as Maud Pember Reeves thought the only sensible way to organise poor families was to stop all this inefficient pottering about at home and communalise tasks such as eating and laundry.

Private Life

In addition to inclinations to Utopian solutions, most social commentators who look into the future have tended to underestimate the passionate adherence to private life—at the cost of any amount of 'efficiency'. The advertisers in *Woman and Home* magazine have got it right: most women place great importance on having their very own kitchen, organised in their very own way, with their very own crockery and casseroles and labour-saving devices. People may yearn for community in a sense of attachment to place and a network of family and friends; but they are deeply attached to private life when it comes to hearth and home. All Utopians ignore or under-estimate that. When Bertrand and Dora Russell said that traditional sexual relations were 'only' like property, they revealed how disastrously they misunderstood the average individual's yearning for their very own piece of property, even be it an allotment patch; and by the same token, perhaps, indeed, their very own partner for life.

Confidence in Marriage

Jessie Bernard did see that the 'permissive society' appealed to men more than to women; consistently more men said they would like to indulge in 'wife-swapping' than women wanted to indulge in 'husband-swapping'. Again, like so many 'optimists', she thought this might change with the passage of time, when the values of the younger generation were better established.

It is true of course, that more liberal mores are established today in that, for example, divorce and remarriage are no longer a cause for scandal; since one-third of children are now born out of wedlock, there is no longer (I think rightly) a stigmat-isation of 'illegitimacy'. But whereas most optimists of the past, in the mainstream, have believed that change would be better and marriage could be saved, what seems to be happening in our time is that the younger generation today have lost hope about marriage. They have not lost all confidence: but if we judge behaviour by what people do rather than by what they say, we can see everywhere the same patterns. The increase in cohabitation rather than marriage because of the distrust of marriage; the increase in divorce and separation (for cohabitation turns out to be even less stable than marriage); the increase in single parenting. (Never-married women are now the fastest-growing group claiming welfare.)

In other words, it seems that many women have interpreted, and acted upon, the thesis offered by radical feminists of the 1960s and 1970s—that marriage is historically a conspiracy to control and repress women, and to treat them like slaves.

Women and Family Power

How curious it is, then, that historically, despite some of the draconian legal conditions of marriage (for women), it was *women*, down the ages who upheld marriage, sought it for their daughters, made marriage arrangements and laid down rituals of courtship. The London 'season', as revealed by Leonore Davidoff in *The Best Circles*, was, since the beginning, a matriarchal plot to ensure that their daughters met appropriate young men. American women, who, since the 19th century have been regarded as the most emancipated (and probably have been better treated than women anywhere else in the world) were merely shocked that in England the matriarchs 'allowed' the menfolk to turn to grouse-shooting and other field sports as a relief from the ardours of the season. The American matriarchs *disapproved* of men being given the social freedom to organise sporting events that took them out of the realm of the matriarchal power and control.

Everywhere we look at marriage and family organisation, we notice that it is women who, historically, underline the importance of stable family life; and wherever women achieve personal power, we will frequently find a dynastic system behind them.

It is the proud boast of Irish historians that women held more power, and enjoyed more rights, under the ancient Celtic laws—known as the Brehon laws—than they did under Anglo-Norman, and later British rule. This is also said to be the case in Scandinavia, where Norse law favoured female rule more than later, feudal 'European' law. In the early Saxon Christian period in England, we find a flowering of powerful female talent in the church—abbesses like Etheldreda and Ethelburga and Hilda of Whitby wielded power and exercised authority, not uncommonly as the head of double monasteries (of men and women) and not uncommonly as part of a family pattern. The headships of abbeys and convents not unusually passed from mother to daughter (since widows frequently retired to convents) or from aunt to niece.

What ancient Celtic society, ancient Norse society and early Christian England have in common is that they are familial, dynastic societies. No doubt they were 'male chauvinist' in that these were warrior cultures: raping and pillage was, after all, the Norse way of life when it came to invasions. Yet women derived power from family power, not merely because it was 'given' under such systems: but because it seems that women gain confidence and personal authority within a dynastic system.

Indeed, it seems that where there is no family system, women seek to recreate one: 'women turn office life into a family,' says Deirdre McSharry, the launching editor of *Cosmopolitan* magazine in Britain, and one of the most successful and experienced of magazine editors. Office relationships become 'family' relationships, as various individuals come to represent the benign aunt, the encouraging (or controlling) mother, the competitive sibling, the wise (or repressive) father with the purse-strings (since 'management' is often male, even in female-dominated organisations).

Thus, while all developed societies are 'patriarchal' in legalistic structure, is it not likely that in substance much of organised society is 'matriarchal'—and familial? Is it not possible, too, that dynastic systems have been based on an unconscious 'deal', whereby men have been awarded the legalistic power while women have so much of the emotional and psychological control? For if marriage 'services' men, the family 'services' women in that it seems to provide women with a power-base in which they can fulfil their irrepressible desire for motherhood, their feeling for networks and kin, and even, perhaps, a backdrop for the development of the feminine personality.

American research on divorce indicates[9] that for many men, a continuous relationship to their children depends upon their being married to the children's mothers: American and British figures are similar in reporting that divorced fathers have a high rate of failure to pay child support (around 50 per cent of divorced fathers do not): and a high rate of failing to keep in continuous touch with the child. For many men, the children are 'over' when the marriage is over. This will be linked to many other factors—such as remarriage, or indeed custodial practice which nearly always leans towards the mother. But it remains the case that fathers are consistently more distant from childcare than mothers.

The Benefits of Patriarchy

The folk-game which begins: 'The farmer wants a wife: the wife wants a child' may indeed have a solid basis in human social organisation. Men want women, women want children (and children want hamsters). If patriarchy was designed to 'control' women, then matriarchy was developed to 'ensnare' men. If men are to have a stake in domestic society, it seems, they must be given something in return, and what they were given, perhaps, is 'patriarchy'. In our generation, we have torn down patriarchy, considering it something bad, inimical to equality, even indeed to human rights. Unsurprisingly, this has hugely contributed to an increase in crime and social dislocation: 70 per cent of men in American state penitentiaries were brought up in fatherless homes. Patriarchy can disappear, leaving only raw male chauvinism behind.

As the work of Joanna Bourke[10] has shown, historically women have often chosen domesticity in preference to work outside the home precisely because it gave them more power, more authority, more freedom and more fulfilment. The family has so often been woman's power-base out of choice, not coercion. There is much evidence to suppose that G.K. Chesterton was correct when he wrote:

> Of the two sexes the woman is in the more powerful position. For the average woman is at the head of something with which she can do as likes; the average man has to obey orders and do nothing else. He has to put one dull brick on another dull brick, and do nothing else; he has to add one dull figure to another dull figure, and do nothing else. The woman's world is a small one, perhaps, but she can alter it ... The woman does work which is in some small degree creative and individual.[11]

Many women have seen home-making that way, and domesticising as a creative niche of civilisation. Today, we would say that this is all very well for some women but people must be given the choice. Yes, single childless people always have the choice about how much to invest in domestic life, but once there are children, the picture is immutably changed.

Women will always want children and most mothers, in the end, come to the view that the family is the best cradle of all. Marriage depends on women, perhaps, more than men: women seem to carry more of the health and emotional burdens of the yoke, and they seem to expect more from it too—women seek divorce because they are less willing than men to put up with a dissatisfying marriage. But children and family life seem to give more back to women too if we judge by the way in which women, everywhere, have sought to turn family life into a matriarchy.

Notes

1 Kramarae, C. and Treichler, P.A. (eds.), *A Feminist Dictionary*, London: Pandora, 1985.

2 Brown, G., *The Decay of Marriage*, Family Education Trust, 1991.

3 See also Hafner J., *The End of Marriage: Why Monogamy Isn't Working*, Century, 1993.

4 'Why Divorce is Grounds for a Health Warning', *Daily Mail*, 16 November 1991.

5 Mallett, P., 'Women and Marriage in Victorian Society', in *Marriage and Property*, Craik, E.M., (ed.), Aberdeen University Press, 1984.

6 Birkett, J., 'Marriage, Divorce and the French Revolution', in Craik, *op. cit.*

7 Bernard, J., *The Future of Marriage*, Souvenir Press, 1972.

8 Dominian, J. *et al.*, *Marital Breakdown and the Health of the Nation*, London: One Plus One, 1991.

9 Whitehead, B.D., 'Dan Quayle Was Right', *The Atlantic Monthly*, May 1993, p. 62.

10 Joanna Bourke's research reveals that working-class women in Britain and Ireland eagerly chose to become housewives in the late 19th and early 20th century. See *Working-Class Culture 1890-1970*, London: Routledge, 1993. Also *Husbandry to Housewifery: Women, Economic Change and Housework in Ireland 1890-1914*, Oxford: Clarendon Press, 1993.

11 Essay on 'Woman', in *The Essential G.K. Chesterton*, Oxford University Press, 1987.

Justice and Liberty in Marriage and Divorce

Norman Barry

In Britain there are over 150,000 divorces a year, 30 per cent of all marriages fail, one in two second marriages fail, and one in five children under the age of 16 will have divorced parents. In addition, one in four children is now born out of wedlock (though often of 'stable relationships'). In some parts of the Western world the figures are, if anything, slightly worse. In the US one in two marriages can be expected to fail, with similarly declining longevity of remarriages. Australia which has had perhaps the most lax (I do not use the word 'liberal', for reasons which will become apparent) divorce laws in the West since 1975 has experienced similar rises in marital breakdown. The emergence of single-parent families, either as a consequence of divorce or from the attractions of unmarried motherhood, has disturbed policy-makers.

One reason is purely economic: the alarming increase in welfare costs brought about by the decline in the traditional family unit. The autonomy and self-sufficiency of this form of living, which is essential for the sustaining of a free society of independent individuals and families, is obviously threatened by the inexorable rise in single-parent households: the annual costs of which have risen to a staggering £4 billion in scarcely more than a decade. This phenomenon has been caused by both the increase in unmarried motherhood and the costs associated with the increase in divorce (largely due to both the inadequacy of maintenance payments and the failure to enforce them). The costs, however, are not simply measurable in terms of state welfare spending. Many critics[1] now maintain that the decay in social morality that we are witnessing and the corroding of traditional institutions have much wider, though related, implications. Some have to do with long-term economic considerations and focus on the fact that economic prosperity in the West (and elsewhere) has been associated with the stable family unit. Others are concerned more directly with moral issues, most noticeably the decline in personal responsibility for action which is said to have been brought about by permissive family and divorce laws.

There is, however, an additional moral question which is likely to become increasingly more pressing: that is the justice of the divorce laws themselves. It is a common view that justice and fairness have no place in matrimonial matters; that the cold formalism that they represent is irrelevant, if not actually harmful, to the emotionally-charged atmosphere of divorce proceedings. This view would appear to be reflected in the development of matrimonial law in Western societies where notions of 'blame' and 'fault' have been almost eliminated not only from the question of the grounds for the dissolution of a marriage but, more importantly, from the terms of the 'ancillaries' or settlement itself, i.e. the arrangements for the custody of children and the division of property. Along with this is the tendency for 'conciliation' between potentially warring spouses to replace adversarial processes (which are traditionally concerned with the authoritative determination of right and wrong).

Attitudes to Marriage

It should be noted that marriage remains a popular arrangement although people are marrying at a slightly older age.[2] Even though in both Britain and America the chance of marital success will *decrease* with succeeding marriages the *idea* of permanent matrimonial union is as alluring as ever. Indeed, the well-attested phenomenon of divorced women re-marrying at a slightly lower rate than divorced men is surely better explained by economic factors, e.g. the fact that married women normally retain custodial rights over children reduces their attractiveness as potential partners (as does the fact, especially in America, of their reduced economic circumstances), than it is by any emotionally-based disinclination for the married state. All social

39

surveys have clearly revealed that the household headed by a married couple remains people's ideal. However, their *behaviour* clearly belies this: indeed it indicates that formal marriage, with all its obligations and responsibilities, has become one of a range of choices of life-styles rather than an arrangement of overwhelming moral importance. This difference between what people profess to believe about marriage and how they actually behave is analogous to the case of citizens *expressing* a desire for expanded public services and a willingness to pay for them in higher taxes (as revealed in opinion surveys) *and* their reluctance to vote for governments to do precisely these things. Costless morality would seem to be a universal human desire.

Despite the evidence of public opinion surveys our attitudes to marriage have undoubtedly changed. The important question here is the explanation for this. What was once viewed as a binding commitment, to be enjoyed or endured, has tended to become a provisional agreement, to be terminated at the whim of both or either of two parties. Furthermore, its significance as an indissoluble union of a man and woman has increasingly come to be challenged: hence the demand for homosexual 'marriage', which has actually been acknowledged in some jurisdictions. Thus the solemnity of the marriage vow has been badly compromised by the ease with which its burdens can be repudiated and by the diminution of its special significance as a unique union between the sexes.

Whether the dramatic changes in marriage that we have witnessed represent a genuine change in the public perception of the institution, and in the force of the moral duties that it involves, or that changes in the divorce law (and in the distribution of costs and benefits that the dissolution of marriage involves) are more significant is a difficult question. Evidence from America suggests that the introduction of 'no fault' divorce law in almost all of the states of the Union since the 1970s brought only a slight increase in the divorce rate.[3] It seems that there attitudes had already sufficiently changed so that legal innovations were simply responses to the public mood. However, in Britain it certainly cannot be denied that the passage of the 1969 Divorce Reform Act (and subsequent legislation) was a significant factor in the rapid increase in marital breakdown. An important point here (to be considered below) is not merely the *de facto* elimination of fault from the grounds of divorce itself but also its (almost, but not quite) removal from the conditions governing the post-divorce settlement. It is here that the demands of justice (scarcely honoured at all in current divorce law) may well compete with the desire for personal liberty. The evidence would seem to be that however 'moral' people would like to be with regard to marriage, the incentive structures facing couples are unlikely to encourage the preservation of that morality.

The facts of marital breakdown do suggest that there has been a change in the *meaning* of marriage in the contemporary world: a change that has been highlighted by the growth of a new spirit of liberty (at least in social matters): a belief that individuals should be the autonomous makers of their own lives, and should not be confined by traditional rules and practices, however advantageous these might be for social stability. This is no doubt partly a consequence of the greater participation of women in the workforce; a fact which must go some way towards explaining why it is that, in most Western countries, women are disproportionately the instigators of divorce proceedings. Any attempt to revert to traditional *roles* with regard to marriage would badly compromise the newly-won independence of women.

Marriage as a Vow

In the history of marriage we can see two competing concepts at work: marriage as a vow and as a contract. The connections between marriage and divorce on the one hand, and liberty and justice on the other cannot be understood without an understanding of vows and contracts.

To put it simply, a marriage vow is a binding and solemn commitment, under either canon or civil law. It is specifically addressed to the subjectivist notion of morality as a matter of personal choice, and, in relation to marriage, it presupposes that the permanent union of a man and woman represents a higher, objective ethic. It follows from this that no marriage can be revocable at the mere whim of the parties, even if there is mutual agreement between them, since the taking of a vow specifically precludes that subjectivity. The philosopher Hegel put the matter well in his claim that no moral community could be constructed out of the subjective choices of individuals alone (even when subject to law) and in his argument that a purely empirical conception of liberty (i.e. as the absence of constraint) is destructive of social order. A marriage vow imposes an unavoidable limitation on our desires for the purpose of achieving a higher organic union, which, in effect, releases the partners from the constraints of their merely ephemeral and subjective desires: 'their union is a self-restriction, but in fact it is their liberation because in it they attain their substantive self-consciousness'.[4] From this perspective, it is easy to see why Hegel should attach such importance to the wedding *ceremony*, for this symbolises the depth of the renunciation of subjective desire in the way that a formal agreement or contract never can.

This does not mean that a marriage may never be dissolved. Those who believe that marriage is a vow may admit to circumstances in which the union has become meaningless, that the partners cannot achieve any objective morality by its continuation. But the important point here is that the decision as to whether these conditions are met ought not to be that of the partners, that would be to surrender to the caprice of subjectivism, but it should be the objective conclusion of a disinterested third party[5] (the Church or the state). The Catholic church goes further when it maintains that a marriage can never be dissolved but only annulled, i.e. deemed never to have been a 'marriage' in the proper sense of the word.

Before dismissing all this as a piece of heady, organic metaphysics which has no place in a largely individualistic Western world, in which such a high premium is placed on personal autonomy, it must be recognised that, in a confused way, the public does regard, in theory at least, marriage as representative of a form of union qualitatively different from a mere agreement or contract. If it is a contract it is *meant* to be a permanent one; almost as a kind of protection from the instability, and ephemeral nature of, private desires. Indeed, the well-attested fact that many people come to regret their divorces suggests that the relentless subjectivism of the modern liberal state may have destructive effects.[6] The fact that suicide rates, depression and alcoholism are much higher in divorced couples (leaving aside the adverse effects on children) further supports the view of cultural conservatives that individualism is a false god that punishes especially harshly those who choose to live by its tenets. At the very least, the onerous conditions imposed on individuals by the concept of marriage as a vow is a pointed reminder that morality does not come easily to individuals, that we may require something outside ourselves to help us to realise ourselves fully. This can only be more or less intransigent and restrictive law.

Marriage as a Contract

The rival conception of marriage as a contract between two parties which can ultimately be repudiated has, of course, come to dominate Western thought, principally because it is more consonant with individualism. It is, though, still recognised to be a special sort of contract, not directly analogous to commercial contracts. This is not merely because of the existence of children (relationships between parents and children, and the obligations involved here, surely cannot be subsumed under the notion of contract), it is also because 'society' still seems to accept that the emotional aspects of marriage prevent the problems associated with it being resolved by the cold, formality of law. Marriage contracts are expected to be permanent and not to be repudiated at will, however much people's behaviour belies this.

As Ferdinand Mount observes in his history of the family,[7] the idea of marriage as a contract predates Christianity and is an enduring feature of civilised society. It is indeed consonant with many features of Christianity. According to Mount, the idea of marriage as an unbreakable vow was a kind of mutation out of original Christian thought. It was, in fact, an example of the capture of the individual by a church-state hierarchy and it condemned people to permanent misery by its rigorous condemnation and prevention of divorce. This tyranny was neither necessary to society, nor even Christianity, since all civilised societies have granted the right to divorce and to some form of compensation to injured parties should it occur. That divorce was not antithetical to sincere Christians is attested to by John Milton's famous polemic against repressive marriage laws.[8] His view stressed the essential *privacy* of love and marriage and he railed against the Church and the state for attempting to convert and distort the personal experiences of individuals for public purposes. The prohibition of divorce was simply an expression of *power*. In Milton's theory, wanton subjectivism is severely qualified by a commitment to legal procedures that would make appropriate, and predictable, arrangements for the victims of a dissolution of marriage.

The fact that the original theory of marriage as a contract was outrageously sexist, in that rarely were women given the right to terminate unilaterally a marriage, should not distract the modern reader from the basic point: that marriage must ultimately be understood in terms of the private satisfactions that it gives individuals; satisfactions which are not readily available outside the marital state. Thus, the marriage as a contract theory normally distinguishes marriage from a mere private arrangement between consenting adults. It is the *public*, and most often secular, recognition of the more or less permanent (but not necessarily irrevocable) nature of the marriage contract that distinguishes it from a mere commercial contract. No subjective choices, however intensely felt, can reproduce that particular public validation which distinguishes a marriage from two partners amicably living together. However, this concession to anti-individualism should not be understood as a retreat into the marriage as a vow theory; for the contract, however onerous, and however much it depends upon public validation, is still a product of private desires and its dissolution does not depend upon the intervention of third parties.

What it does have in common with ordinary commercial contracts is the idea of justice. A commercial contract is not irrevocable but when a contract is revoked the disappointment of legitimate expectations which that action involves justifies compensation. Breach of contract is a primary type of injustice. The predictability of a commercial order could not be guaranteed if compensation were not paid for breach of contract. It would indeed be meaningless. The theory of marriage as a contract involves a similar notion of justice, even though the personal and emotional commitments that marriage involves are perhaps not fully justiciable: feelings are clearly not exchangeable goods. Nevertheless, the kinds of investments that people make in marriage, in terms of property and the efforts involved in the nurturing of children, are comprehensible within a theory of justice that confines itself to procedural rules of equality and to appropriate forms of compensation for those 'victimised' by the breach of the basic features of the marital contract (though this may be extraordinarily difficult to demonstrate).

Historically, the theory of marriage as a contract has triumphed precisely because it meets with the rise of individualism and the secularisation of modern life. Like it or not, personal liberty and autonomy have become irresistible demands and to pretend otherwise (in law or morality) is simply to encourage hypocrisy. People will break their vows and the tolerance of such breaches will eventually lead to a degrading of the vow itself. An example may be seen in the most extreme form of the vow: the Catholic marriage which can only be annulled. All sorts of casuistry (and hypocrisy) have been used by Catholics anxious to end their marriages so that the concept of annulment has on occasions been simply degraded. What was or was not a genuine marriage turns on the subjective opinion of the Catholic hierarchy. Prominent Catholic public figures seem to have little difficulty in getting annulments. Indeed, during the debate in Ireland leading up to the (unsuccessful) referendum asking the population whether they wished divorce to be permitted, some devout Catholics actually said that it should because the ease with which annulments could be obtained was itself making a mockery of the idea of indissoluble marriage.

The Meaning of Marriage Today

The most obvious feature of marriage in Western societies is that it is neither a vow nor a contract. Although people may express a desire for the solemnity of a formal arrangement that distinguishes it from an informal partnership terminable at will, the latter is precisely what it has become. The most important fact here is not merely the ease with which a marriage may be dissolved but that the settlement normally bears no relationship to the behaviour of the parties to the original contract. This is a clear contrast with commercial law. Conduct has not only been *de facto* eliminated as a ground for divorce but it also has little relevance to decisions about the custody of children and the division of property.

45

Obviously, the needs of children should be ranked higher than the 'rights' of the partners (a necessary modification to the theory of marriage as a contract) but there is no reason within liberal theory why the contractual elements should be eliminated elsewhere. Justice sometimes may have to give way to other values in the marriage relationship but it does not follow at all from correct liberal theory that it should be discarded entirely, even though the law deals with the most sensitive and emotionally-charged aspects of our lives. It is a curious irony in contemporary liberal social theory that it should on the one hand demand the autonomy of individuals, and celebrate their rights to realise themselves as rational agents, yet, on the other, it permits a retreat into *sentimentality* in its analysis of perhaps the most important choice, i.e. that of a marriage partner, that individuals are likely to make.

It is strange, too, that justice, that most favoured of liberal concepts, should have received so little attention in (with one exception, to be considered below), and so little application to, marriage. The lacuna in liberal theory here may partly be because of the current concern for 'social' rather than procedural justice.

Indeed, the current obsession with 'conciliation' as the method for resolving differences between partners is deliberately contrasted favourably with legal adjudication. Progressive thinkers would appear to prefer a form of social therapy to the authoritative determination of right and wrong. This has been taken to extremes in Australia which has perhaps the most permissive divorce law in the West (Family Law Act, 1975). There, Family Courts have virtually dispensed with formal notions of legality and have decided disputes between spouses on the vaguest and most indeterminate of grounds. This has naturally led to unpredictability; which is perhaps the most damaging shortcoming a legal system can have. In fact conciliation is a primitive rather than a progressive notion precisely because it dispenses with the ideas of right, wrong, and personal responsibility for action.

Marriage and Liberty

In Western countries the law regarding marriage has become extremely permissive, perhaps more so than individuals would like. In particular, it has brought about a perversion of the moral ideal of liberty. Originally, the moral right to liberty was based upon the notion of personal responsibility for action. Individuals are treated as free agents capable of making rational choices because of their awareness of, and responsibility for, the consequences of their choices. In traditional liberal theory a person's moral development is very largely a function of a learning process in which he or she has to pay the costs of the mistakes that so often flow from the exercise of freedom. In theory, the idea of a society based on contract is not at all permissive precisely because contracts are onerous, they place burdens on the parties which they cannot easily cast aside. Liberty consists in the fact that contracts are freely made. Of course, free choice and personal responsibility are not limited to contracts but include any form of voluntary action in which costs can be more or less known. However, in modern Western society the state has gradually absorbed the costs that accrue when individuals make mistakes. Hence the rise of the one-parent families, the increase in marital breakdown and other undesirable social phenomena which are encouraged by permissive laws and easily-available welfare.

Good Intentions and British Law

The noticeable fact in all this is that the gradual disintegration of personal responsibility began with good intentions, which would have been approved of by John Milton. Prior to 1969 many married couples in Britain were trapped in unhappy marriages which presumably were of little benefit to their children, let alone themselves. The necessity of proving a marital offence to secure a divorce meant that couples who would have voluntarily agreed to separate had either to endure their misery or engage in collusive activity (which itself brought about disrespect for the law). However, the terms of the divorce settlement were directly related to the conduct that led to the divorce so that at least a strong concept of personal responsibility for action remained.

The 1969 Act,[9] by introducing the concept of the 'irretrievable breakdown' of a marriage (although it did not entirely remove the notion of fault or conduct) at least opened the way for a more civilised and less hypocritical approach to divorce. There are now five possible conditions for the demonstration of irretrievable breakdown: mutual agreement after a two-year separation, adultery, unreasonable behaviour, desertion for at least two years and unilateral renunciation of the marriage after a five-year separation. Of course there is still some chicanery involved if couples require a 'quickie' divorce since then one of the fault-based reasons for irretrievable breakdown has to be invoked.

Courts have been remarkably lax in their interpretation of unreasonable behaviour (which has to be sufficiently objectionable to make it impossible for the petitioner to live with his or her spouse). Although the courts have the authority to refuse to grant a divorce even when the petition is undefended, this is rarely exercised. They have not regarded it as their duty to protect the sanctity of marriage even when the complaint might be regarded as trivial. Thus we do have *de facto* divorce on demand in this country.

Lawyers have worried about some of the legal processes involved in all this but for conservatives this is not the real problem. The connection between liberty and personal responsibility was broken through developments in the common law, which were later embodied in statute. The key case is *Wachtel v. Wachtel* (1973)[10] in which it was ruled by the judges at both the lower court and on appeal that conduct should not normally be relevant to the ancillaries. Echoing the prevailing 'liberal' sentiment, Lord Denning, the Master of the Rolls, wrote that 'the court should not reduce its order for financial provision merely because of what was formerly regarded as guilt or blame. To do so would be to impose a fine for supposed misbehaviour in the course of an unhappy married life'.[11] The courts officially declared their incompetence to penetrate the secrets of a marriage in order to attribute blame or to allocate responsibility for its failure. With the qualification that, except where it is 'both obvious and gross', conduct should not be taken into account, the courts, under the precedent established under *Wachtel*, were led to ignore questions of right and wrong, justice and injustice. Under later statute law,[12] conduct which is so gross that not to consider it would be 'inequitable' is supposed to be relevant but this provision appears towards the end of a list of facts appropriate to the ancillaries. It has rarely been invoked.

It is then quite inaccurate to describe marriage as a contract since no adverse consequences are visited upon those who breach its terms. Again, it is impossible to describe the freedoms that legal changes have introduced as emanations out of traditional liberal or conservative doctrine since the new liberties are almost completely detached from any notion of personal responsibility for action. Thus, although it is true that some conservatives[13] have blamed the rise of permissiveness, the disintegration of the family and the devaluation of the institution of marriage on the rise of a contract-based society and individualistic order devoid of communal, moral obligations, their argument misrepresents the traditional liberal position. A contract-based society is not amoral or uncontrollably egoistic even though the duties that characterise it are largely self-assumed. The changes in matrimonial law, both in common law and statute, that have occurred were specifically designed to remove the notion of moral responsibility for action in marriage. It is, then, the institutions of the state that have been the trail-blazers in the rise of permissiveness.

Divorce, Permissiveness and the Law

Britain has been little different from the rest of the world in the eagerness of its legislators and judges to remove justice and personal responsibility from matrimonial law. However, it may be doubted that these innovations represent a genuine change in public opinion with regard to moral conduct. One suspects that the taste for adultery and other forms of marital misconduct is pretty much constant over time. What has changed, however, is the incentive structure that now faces potentially erring spouses. One does not have to be a soulless economic determinist to suggest that costs and benefits have an influence on human behaviour. It is naïve to argue that proper moral conduct can be sustained without a legal framework that at least sets the terms for that conduct.

There are, of course, other reasons than legal changes which can explain the rise in the divorce rate.[14] The increase in the employment of women undoubtedly makes a difference to the economics of the household since it alters the division of labour between the partners: the wife is no longer confined to performing household tasks and the husband is not the sole

49

generator of income. Thus the familiar 'gains from trade' that accrue from marriage are less readily available. Again, one would expect lower divorce rates among married couples with children than those without since the latter have not normally accumulated valuable marital 'capital' which is worth preserving. The fact that divorce is more likely within the first five years of marriage than later hardly requires explanation. All these propositions are well-established, and the behaviour they describe is affected by changes in the external constraints that are faced by married couples. However, similar accurate predictions could be made about the behaviour of couples who were not actually married but living together.

The issue that concerns most critical observers of contemporary marriage is primarily moral: it is about the changing status of marriage as a valuable *social* institution that has been generated by the familiar legal innovations. I would suggest that the only way in which marriage can be resuscitated is by reincorporating the idea of justice into its fundamental features. The difficulty is that there is now much disagreement about what justice in marriage means.

Justice, Contracts and Marriage

Justice is relevant to marriage in two distinct but nevertheless inter-related ways. First, the relaxation of the conditions attending divorce has undoubtedly created incentives which encourage family breakdown, to the ultimate costs of society (in terms of increased welfare payments to single-parent families) and perhaps to couples themselves for whom the immediate attractions of divorce are very often followed by long-term unhappiness. Secondly, there is a widespread feeling that ordinary people, if not the 'liberal' elite, feel that human conduct is relevant to the divorce settlement, that some parties are treated unjustly by the law. This is illustrated dramatically in Australia where there have been physical attacks by outraged spouses on Family Court judges. In Britain, the campaign for justice in divorce has largely been led by aggrieved husbands compelled to pay maintenance to ex-wives (or face imprisonment) when they have done no wrong. Of course, wives often feel unjustly treated, especially when, as is often the case, particularly in America, their incomes fall relatively to those of their ex-husbands after divorce.

The restoration of the concept of marriage as a vow is clearly a non-starter. The hypocrisy and misery produced by very traditional marriage rules is quite inappropriate for the socially libertarian times in which we inescapably live. The vow aspect of marriage is now no more than decorative.

The only solution lies in some strengthening of the conventional features of marriage. This can be done in either a radical or a conservative way. The radical way would be to remove almost entirely (but not completely) the state from marriage and allow couples themselves to determine the form of marriage that they wish. They could decide in advance the terms of the contract and the procedures to be entered into if it should be breached. Couples could voluntarily decide, for example, what would happen in the event of either a mutually agreed or unilateral repudiation of the contract. They could, for example, restore adultery to its traditional role in the ancillaries. The state would be reduced to laying down universal obligations for the care of children and other (minor) ancillary conditions. Notice that this is quite different from pre-nuptial agreements that are often made in America. It is a feature of the common law that it is impossible for people to contract out of obligations imposed by a statute so that pre-nuptial agreements are necessarily limited in scope. If, for example, a marital 'offence', such as adultery is no longer, by statute, relevant to the divorce settlement then couples cannot by their own agreement make it so.

This radical version of contractualism has some attractions.[15] On the assumption that individuals are less permissive in their attitudes towards divorce than the state, it is quite likely that voluntary contracts would be more restrictive than the uniform one supplied by the monopoly state. Indeed, in Australia, the disgust felt by people towards the federal divorce law led to the growth of private contracts, often of a quite restrictive kind, which are enforced by the courts. What the parties to these agreements cannot do, though, is call themselves husband and wife.

The advantage of the extreme contractualist approach is that it draws attention to the need for 'pre-commitment', the idea that people would like some guarantee that their own behaviour, as well as that of others, will be restrained by a prior rule. It is a device to protect ourselves from the temptations of the *immediate*; temptations which may lead to long-term harm to ourselves. The fact that many people come to regret their divorces suggests that matters would improve if there were arrangements for pre-commitment. In economic examples, people may wish to supply voluntarily a public good, yet they need some assurance that individuals will not welch on the deal. In the marital context, it is simply the recognition of the fact that individuals need some help in order to be moral. It is obvious that in the marriage law supplied by the state there is an extraordinarily inefficient form of pre-commitment.

Attractive though the radical contractarian model is I do not think that it is appropriate for marriage. The attempt to 'privatise' marriage in this way would be to deprive it of its significance as a social institution, whose public value is created by the approval of citizens, despite their departures from the moral standards that it sets. It is the one virtue of the vow theory of marriage that its stress on the public nature of the institution distinguishes it categorically from mere relationships, however well-protected by contract law. Individuals cannot, by their subjective choices, create marriage; it is a 'given', the value of which derives entirely from the fact it is not a voluntarily created institution (like a company).

This is perhaps why homosexual marriages should be excluded by the state. Their validation would damage what most people perceive to be a genuine public good. Of course, there is nothing in theory to stop homosexual couples making whatever private contracts they wish. Furthermore, since the state will inevitably be involved with important aspects of marriage, such as the care of children, the scope of individualism is necessarily limited.

Restructuring the State Marriage Contract

The restoration of pre-commitment will be better achieved by a rather more conservative solution: the restructuring of the state marriage contract. Only by this can personal liberty (which is denied by the vow theory) and justice be connected. This means that statute law should recognise that the marriage contract creates rights and obligations which must be justiciable: not merely because it is intrinsically right that they should be so but also because only these can provide the elements of pre-commitment which fragile and morally unreliable individuals so clearly need. Thus, while adultery, unreasonable behaviour and so on, need not be the sole grounds for divorce they should certainly feature strongly in the ancillaries. The law, for example, must provide that there should be a presumption (for obvious reasons) in favour of the mother having custody of children, but her claim could be countered, and modified, by clear evidence that her marital behaviour adversely affected her capacity here. However, the courts would make some allowance for a wife's contribution to home-making even if she were adjudged to be at fault.

People who enter marriage have a moral right to expect that marital duties will be performed reasonably and that adverse consequences will be visited on those who disregard them. Hence, if the state regards fidelity as a serious duty of marriage then it is just that spouses should 'pay' for any marital misdemeanour. If the distinguishing feature of marriage is that it is, or should be, a permanent arrangement, then obviously this creates expectations in both parties. To discount such expectations by refusing to admit obvious facts of wrong-doing into disputes over property and maintenance is to undermine the *meaning* of the marriage contract. The legal disputes that now take place on the dissolution of marriage may be fierce but they do not normally involve questions of conduct (although these may implicitly appear). Those who stress that conciliation should replace legalism have only half of the argument. Conciliation is, of course, desirable if reached mutually but not if it is 'imposed' by social workers or counsellors. This is, as the Australian experience shows, likely to lead to unpredictability.

Nothing in these proposed changes would prevent the unilateral repudiation of a marriage (it is not important in principle just how long a marriage should last before this is permissible). However, any spouse that so acts would forego any claim to (personal) maintenance, and the right to a share of the common property of the marriage would be qualified.

It has been suggested[16] that there should be an additional penalty against the wrongful party in a marital dispute: that he or she should be penalised for the withdrawal of that affection which is prescribed by the marriage contract. This seems to be highly contentious. People do not pre-commit themselves to undying love in a marital contract and the withdrawal of that surely cannot be compensated. They merely wish to protect themselves against more easily measurable adverse consequences of a marital break-up.

No doubt the objection to these tentative proposals to restore fully fault to the system of marital law will be that it is impossible to assign misconduct to particular parties, that (as judges and legislators in the 1960s and 1970s argued) marriages break down for a whole congeries of reasons which cannot be reduced to individual conduct. It is claimed that we cannot have the courts prying into the intimate secrets of a marriage. However, the objection derives from the dogma of the permissive era which maintained that nobody is to blame for anything. But as even the current British law grudgingly admits, but rarely applies, sometimes people are to blame: to argue that they are not is to imply that there ought to be freedom without responsibility in marital affairs. It is true that it might be difficult for the courts to assign fault, and that the attempt to do so will often reveal unpleasantness. But these are unfortunate facts of life: not insuperable barriers to the restoration of justice in marriage. In some cases, a breakdown would be mutually agreed so that no unpleasant court battles over fault would ensue.

It would, of course, be possible for couples to make subsidiary contracts within the broad statutory framework that restored the notion of fault. It is here that pre-nuptial contracts would come into play. They would obviously relate to matters concerning the property that is brought into a marriage by one or both parties. The title to this therefore would not be affected by conduct in the marriage.

The Child Support Agency

The current controversy over the working of the Child Support Agency has renewed interest in the concept of justice in marriage. The Agency, which came into operation in 1993, has the laudable aim of tracking down absent fathers and enforcing on them maintenance orders. The main complaint has been that it is more concerned with efficiency than with justice. It has increased the maintenance orders of ex-husbands (who may very well have remarried) rather than pursued non-payers.

A further objection is that the Agency apparently has the authority to over-rule 'clean break' agreements originally negotiated between divorcing spouses. Some husbands have argued that they signed away valuable property rights, usually the equity in the marital home, in order to be freed of future maintenance obligations. It is, of course, true that the law did not permit a 'clean break' with children, but injustices are clearly occurring. Is there not a problem of 'moral hazard' here, i.e. the creation of an incentive for an ex-wife to go to the Child Support Agency to secure maintenance *after* a 'clean break'? The aim of the Agency is clearly to reduce the costs of income support and not the achievement of justice in marriage and divorce.

It is too early to assess all the effects of the new arrangements but it is certain that post-marital bitterness will be intensified. Already there is a demand from aggrieved ex-husbands that original 'clean break' settlements should be renegotiated in the context of new maintenance orders imposed by the Child Support Agency. It is well worth suggesting that the current injustices could have been avoided if fault had been a factor in the original divorce settlements. That would not have removed the obligations of an ex-husband to his children but it would certainly have affected the nature of the 'clean break'.

Justice and 'Social' Justice in Marriage

Feminist critics of my proposals fully to restore fault to the system of marital law might argue that they are subtly designed to favour men over women in marital disputes. Most divorces are initiated by women and in Britain the favoured ground for a 'quickie' divorce is unreasonable behaviour, which is hardly worth defending in the current legal context. It is easy to demonstrate. Today, even if men successfully launch a divorce petition against their wives for adultery (the most popular male ground) or unreasonable behaviour they, since husbands are normally the major income earners, will still have to bear the costs of maintenance and will lose property. Am I not recommending a solution which will restore a *status quo ante* which it is said always favoured men over women? Will it simply encourage a rush of petitions by husbands?

This charge has to be taken seriously. It is supported by the facts that, in America especially, women are worse off financially than men after divorce.[17] Maintenance orders are difficult to enforce (alimony payments tend to be temporary in America so that once the value and division of such things as the house and other assets are settled the husband is more or less free of obligations) and, since women normally have custody of the children, they are less able to participate in the re-marriage market.

Susan Okin[18] has argued that the absence of justice in American marriage means that the law treats women as equals when the conditions of marriage renders them unequal. A crucial point in her argument is that the most important source of family wealth is human capital (normally the husband's future earning power). Since divorced women have a much diluted claim over this in divorce settlements they are (for this and other reasons) unjustly treated by the law. She rightly points out the adverse effects that no fault divorce laws have on women, although she does not see the importance of this in the context of a theory of formal justice.

However, we should treat the fact of a divorced wife's reduced income with a little caution. A person's welfare is by no means solely a function of his or her income. For example, if a wife voluntarily repudiates a marriage then even though she may forego some or all of her husband's future income, she is still better off. She is freed from a presumably irksome husband. Her lowered income is simply a cost she has to bear in order to increase her overall welfare (of which not being married is a part). Under my proposals, if a husband repudiates the marriage he would not be relieved of maintenance costs (which would be rigorously enforced, possibly for a life-time) and his share of property would be proportionate to his fault. Indeed, the existence of fault provisions in the law would put wives in a much stronger bargaining position. The fact that women normally secure custody of children, and hence are likely to have a low standard of living, should not itself justify an automatic redistribution of income from husbands to wives. Some men want custody, even though they normally lose custody battles, and it would be unjust in such cases to insist that husbands should make *extra* payments to ex-wives, except where the man is at fault. The welfare of wives is increased by having custody of children despite their cost. Many men certainly regard themselves in these cases as worse off for not securing custody. Justice would only be achievable in such obviously difficult matters if consideration of conduct were relevant to the proceedings.

It seems to me that Professor Okin does not appreciate the full significance of the fault provision as a *procedural* device for securing justice in marriage. Her claim is that in principle 'both post-divorce households should enjoy the same standard of living'.[19] This, however, is an egalitarian claim that for her should characterise all post-marital relationships, irrespective of conduct. It is justified, apparently on the ground that men's income is normally higher anyway. But can it be just that a husband should be obliged to pay for an erring wife indefinitely? Does a divorced wife have a claim on (possibly unexpected) increases in an ex-husband's income irrespective of the circumstances of the breakdown? It seems to be quite wrong to use the marriage laws as some kind of device to correct the inequalities of income between men and women that may emerge spontaneously from market processes. Professor Okin wishes to create 'social' justice in marriage (and post-marriage) rather than justice.

My agenda would not correct these inequalities but it would certainly reduce the well-being of some men that obtains under the present law. Philandering, and drunken or violent, husbands would have to pay the costs of their behaviour. The rigorous enforcement of maintenance orders would relieve the state of some of the costs of one-parent families. Equally important is the fact that the change in the incentive structure that the reintroduction of fault would entail provides that pre-commitment which is essential if the stability of the family is to be restored. Proposals such as this represent an important repudiation of some of the worst features of the permissive society. This seems to be a more feasible aim than the attempt to introduce a highly contentious egalitarianism into an already complex area.

Notes

1 See Davies, J., (ed.), Berger, B. and Carlson, A., *The Family: Is It Just Another Lifestyle Choice?*, London: Institute of Economic Affairs, 1993.

2 *Marriage and Divorce Statistics 1991: England and Wales*, Series FM2 no. 19, HMSO, 1993.

3 See Becker, G., *A Treatise on the Family*, Cambridge, Mass.: Harvard University Press, 1981, pp. 228-29.

4 Hegel, G.W.F., *The Philosophy of Right*, Translated by W. Knox, Oxford: Clarendon Press, 1952, ch. 4.

5 *Ibid.*, p. 113.

6 See Davis, G. and Murch, M., *Grounds for Divorce*, Oxford: Clarendon Press, 1988, ch. 4.

7 *The Subversive Family*, London: Unwin, 1982.

8 Milton's *The Doctrine and Discipline of Divorce* is discussed in Mount, *op. cit.*, pp. 209-13.

9 For details of British law see Davis and Murch, *op. cit.*; and Glendon, M.A., *The Transformation of Family Law*, Chicago: University of Chicago Press, 1989, ch. 4.

10 See Davis and Murch, *op. cit.*, pp. 14-17.

11 Quoted in Davis and Murch, *op. cit.*, p. 16.

12 Matrimonial and Family Proceedings Act (1984).

13 See Morgan, P., 'Fidelity in the Family: Once Absolute, Now Another "Choice"', in Anderson D., (ed.), *The Loss of Virtue*, London: The Social Affairs Unit, 1993, pp. 99-118.

14 See Becker, *op. cit.*, ch. 10.

15 I took this view once myself, see Barry, N., 'An Individualist's View of Marriage and the Family', *Policy Report*, 1989, pp. 37-39.

16 This seems to be the implication of the argument of Maley, B., *Marriage, Divorce and Family Justice*, Sydney: Centre for Independent Studies, 1993, pp. 38-40, where he suggests that damages should be paid to a wronged party in addition to the claim that the ancillaries should be decided on grounds of fault. This book is, incidentally, a good introduction to the subject and contains useful Australian material.

17 'Separate but Unequal: The Economic Disaster for Women and Children', *Family Law Quarterly*, 1987.

18 *Justice, Gender and the Family*, New York: Basic Books, 1989.

19 *Ibid.*, p. 183.

Biology, Sex Roles and Work

Dr Glenn Wilson

Men and women may be 'equal', but they are not the same. Equality is a political concept, and the legitimate domain of feminism; sex differences are a matter for scientific investigation by psychologists.

To its credit, feminism has opened many doors to women who have traditionally been excluded from certain careers quite unfairly. For some, this has led to a euphoria that perfect gender balance can be achieved in all occupations without biological strain. I do not believe this is the case, because men and women have, on average, different personalities, talents and interests which are rooted in biological (brain and hormonal) differences. Even within the same occupational sphere, their aptitudes are likely to be complementary rather than identical.

Intellectual Differences and Career Choice

First consider intellectual aptitudes. There is now a wealth of evidence that men excel in mathematical and scientific pursuits while women have a slight edge in language skills. These differences can be seen in exam performance at all ages and they are paralleled by differential interest in these areas.[1] The result is that men gravitate toward occupations such as physicist, architect and engineer while women become novelists, journalists and translators.

Despite concerted attempts to over-ride sex-role stereotypes over recent decades, expectations concerning appropriate work roles for men and women emerge very early in life. A recent study by Manchester University[2] found that among boys aged 5–6, 96 per cent thought car repairs should be done only by men, with 90 per cent for woodwork, 85 per cent for fire-fighting, 80 per cent for climbing mountains and 72 per cent for scientists. Girls were slightly less sexist but generally endorsed the same beliefs. Mending clothes, hairdressing, cooking and 'looking after the sick' were seen as women's work. One teacher reported that a child in her class associated sewing with women even though his father was a tailor. Another said that a picture of a woman wearing a white coat and stethoscope was identified as 'a nurse' even by children whose family doctor was female. Apparently these stereotypes are highly resilient.

Some argue that male/female specialisations develop out of childhood stereotypes and social expectations, but this seems very unlikely. The same differences appear in all cultures, including the Israeli kibbutzim where strong efforts were made to override gender differences in development. Little girls learn to talk earlier than boys and the advantage that boys have in spatial ability (for example the capacity to imagine what objects would look like if rotated) shows a dramatic surge at puberty that is apparently related to sex hormone secretion. Female spatial ability varies with the menstrual cycle, also implicating female sex hormones.

The differences in ability are now known to result from differences in brain structure laid down under the influence of hormones during prenatal development.[3] The most striking difference between male and female brains (apart from the fact that male brains are larger) is that male brains are more specialised for spatial processing in the right hemisphere whereas female brains are less clearly lateralized. Female brains, however, appear better equipped for communication between the two hemispheres (having more interconnecting fibres in the middle area called the *corpus callosum*). One result of these differences is that male brains are more susceptible to damage because they have no back-up if something goes wrong in one hemisphere; hence males are more prone to verbal disorders such as stammering, aphasia and dyslexia. However, men are also more likely to show exceptional ability in particular fields such as mathematics and music (for example the levels of genius displayed by Einstein and Mozart).

The differences in ability between average men and women may seem quite small, and the overlap considerable, but they become very important at the upper ends of the distribution, which are likely to be influential in determining career choice and success. For example, above a score of 700 on the American

Scholastic Aptitude Test (Mathematics) there are only 7 per cent females against 93 per cent males.[4]

Although women are moving into certain fields that were once male preserves, it seems most unlikely that gender effects in the work place will ever be totally eliminated. For example, although female representation in the law has doubled over the last decade, female applications for computer science courses have halved.[5] Some male preserves were apparently based on arbitrary convention and vested power, but others almost certainly have a biological foundation.

Personality Traits

Another major difference between typical men and women that has relevance to work is that concerning personality traits such as competitiveness and ambitiousness. Men are typically more motivated than women to devote time and energy to furthering their political and economic position in whatever occupational sphere they choose. The result is that they are inclined to rise in the hierarchy relative to women, a fact which is then put down to discrimination by feminists.

This tendency for males to be more competitive than women is not unique to our society. In 1991 Richard Lynn published a monograph called *The Secret of the Miracle Economy*[6] which reported work motivation measures in 43 countries around the world. Men emerged as more competitive than women in nearly all the countries, as well as placing a higher value on money. The widespread appearance of this sex difference around the world confirms its probable biological origins.

Although women have been admitted in large numbers to previously male occupations such as law and medicine, the top posts are still held mostly by men. Around 95 per cent of bank managers, company directors, judges and university professors in Britain are male. There are few women in the American Senate, the Russian parliament or the British Cabinet. With the notable exception of Mrs Thatcher, nearly all the women in the world who have become national leaders inherited the position from husbands, fathers or other dynastic connections (e.g. Benazir Bhutto, Mrs Bandanaraike, Indira Ghandi, Golda Meir, Eva Perón, Cory Aquino).

The Nobel Prize list is also revealing. While fifteen women have been awarded prizes for literature and peace, there have been only nine in science since the awards began in 1901, at least three of these being for work done in collaboration with their husbands (Marie Curie, Irene Joliot-Curie and Gerti Cori.)[7]

Some element of male discrimination may be involved, but there is no necessary reason to assume it given the extent of cut-throat competition *between* men. What is clear is that dominance is a personality characteristic determined by male hormones.[8] An example of evidence supporting this fact is the finding that aggressive behaviour emerges spontaneously in male monkeys raised by surrogate (inanimate) mothers to a much greater degree than it does in females. And in a study of my own, male finger-length patterns (presumably laid down by hormones) were associated with assertiveness within a group of women.[9] In other words, there are individual differences in masculinity among women that predict male-type personality traits. Of course, assertiveness is not always a good thing; in extremis it results in psychopathy and criminal violence—both of which are much more characteristic of men than women.

Interestingly, all this competitive struggling among men is probably ultimately determined by the evolutionary need to impress women, in order to mate successfully with them. The usual pattern in the animal world is for males to engage in competitive struggles which determine breeding privileges, and a small proportion of males (those emerging at the top of the hierarchy) account for most of the copulations. Not only does prenatal testosterone (the key male hormone) cause competitive aggressiveness, but the experience of triumph releases further testosterone. Following a male tournament (for example a Wimbledon final) the victor is prepared for sexual capitalisation by an increase of male hormone, while the vanquished male's brain chemicals show a change towards those seen in depressed patients. Female sexual responsiveness, by contrast, is enhanced by the sense of being overpowered.[10]

Another possible model for male achievement is the New Guinea bower bird, which depends upon elaborate and impressive constructions (made from any highly coloured articles that can be pilfered) in order to attract a female for mating. This kind of courtship-motivated industry seems to have parallels in the Taj Mahal or the expensive jewellery that wealthy men like Aristotle Onassis are able to provide for their women.

Motivation and Achievement

None of this is to say that women cannot achieve, just that the motivation to do so is greater for the average man. Also female accomplishment when it is observed is more likely to be within the field of interpersonal relationships (for example Florence Nightingale, Mother Teresa and Alva Myrdal). The difference between men and women in this respect can be seen clearly in the attributes that are most valued in a partner by men and women respectively. Whereas men seek attractive, affectionate and socially skilled women, women are looking for achievement and leadership in men, and this may be a female route to power. It is no accident that although the greater part of American wealth is owned by women, it was obtained by inheritance and divorce settlements more often than their own business achievement. Similarly, a recently published list of the 50 richest women in Britain gave nearly all their occupations as heiress, widow, divorcee or wife. Only seven had made their fortunes from business or arts.[11]

The assertion that women are under-promoted relative to their true value is difficult to sustain in the light of empirical research. For example, within the academic profession (at least in the US) men are more productive than their female colleagues at each status/salary level, as measured by number of research publications and citations.[12] This finding holds true even for unmarried, childless women. In other words, objectively speaking, women may already be over-promoted. When the Association of University Teachers in Britain recently reported that women lecturers were discriminated against as regards salary and status,[13] they were able to do so only by excluding all measures of productivity.

A recent study by Beverly Steffert of the University of London found that female students took, on average, twice as long as males to complete funded PhD degrees.[14] This was despite gaining more help from staff members with matters such as statistical analysis. Interestingly, those who were highest in femininity were least likely to finish, again suggesting the male emphasis on achievement.

Of course, women are more likely to have conflicting family and childcare obligations than men. They are also likely to have different priorities, being less concerned with money, prestige and power and devoting their efforts more towards fostering smooth personal relationships and institutional service. Indeed, surveys show that women do value aspects of work other than straightforward achievement and output. A recent MORI poll conducted for the GMB union found that male workers were more concerned than females about pay, fringe benefits and opportunities for advancement whereas women placed higher priority on having an interesting and enjoyable job, with flexible hours and working for a boss they could respect. Compared with women, men have a kind of tunnel-vision aimed at power and dominance. They strive to win, even at the expense of friendships, time and physical health.

In his book *Feminism and Freedom*, Michael Levin[15] describes the case of a prominent US Company (one of the so-called 'Fortune 500') that was attacked for not promoting enough women to management positions. This dismayed the company chiefs because they had prided themselves on a policy of strong affirmative action, going out of their way to favour women for corporate advancement. So they hired some research analysts (Hoffmann Associates) to find out what was going wrong. After weeks of study Hoffman concluded that the difference in promotion rate was due entirely to motivation. Women clerks were less ready to relocate or work longer hours and were less inclined to see their jobs as the first rung on a corporate ladder and 44 per cent said they would prefer a part-time job (twice the figure among male clerks). Work was seen as important, but not so consumingly all-important as it was for men. Women were not prepared to make the sacrifices to their other interests that promotion to the top would necessitate.

Even when women do reach the top they may be ambivalent about their achievement when they recognise what they have sacrificed. Joanna Foster, a former head of the British Equal Opportunities Commission, was quoted as follows:

American women climbed up the career ladder fast; but when they got to the boardroom they looked around and saw that all the men had pictures of their families on their desks. The women didn't have any pictures of their families. They didn't have any families ....[16]

Of course there are always going to be some women who are just as independent, aggressive, competitive and risk-taking as any man and they do rise to top management positions. Research indicates that they often have a childhood background of highly active, tomboyish behaviour of the kind that clinical studies show may be induced by their mothers taking male hormones during pregnancy. Thus the women who succeed against male criteria may have brains that are masculinized in certain respects, and hence are more like men in personality.

The gender difference in the relative importance placed on achievement and social relationships is strikingly illustrated by American psychologists Nelson Cowan and George Davidson, who asked people to describe their most salient childhood memories.[17] When these were classed as relating to issues of *competence* (e.g. ability to perform skills, pass exams, succeed in sport) versus *attachment* (please teachers and parents, keep friends, etc.) it was found that men were three times as likely to relate competence memories as attachment, and vice versa for women. That these events occurred in childhood suggests that motivational differences between the sexes begin early.

Sex Differences in Social Relationships

As a matter of fact, sex differences in social interest can be observed within a few days of birth, with little girls paying more attention to, and smiling more, in response to patterns resembling a human face relative to abstract patterns, which to little boys are of equal interest. At the toddler stage, boys and girls react differently to a physical barrier preventing them from reaching their toys. Girls tend to stand at the barrier and cry, while boys are rather more resourceful, trying to find a way round it.[18]

Linked with the value women put on attachment, they are usually superior to men with respect to social communication skills.[19] For example, women tend to be better at reading the non-verbal signals of emotion (what is often called 'body language'). They are better at recognising unspoken messages between people in social situations and in describing the emotions represented by postural stick drawings.

This superior social perceptiveness is commonly referred to as 'women's intuition'. It seems to be partly innate and has probably evolved out of a need to sequester helpful mates and educate offspring. The female ability to decipher non-verbal signals and assess the significance of small details is one of the reasons men find it so hard to lie to their wives. It may also be one of the reasons why women are so interested in crime and detective stories, and write them so well (for example Agatha Christie and Ngaio Marsh). But though women are better at decoding non-verbal signals they are also more transparent in the sending of them. That is, women are more expressive and men relatively 'poker-faced'.

Although partly innate, female intuition is honed by bringing up young children, since non-verbal channels of communication must be used for the first few years. Indeed the experience of dealing with the needs and wiles of young children may equip women particularly well as negotiators, and this may have occupational applications.

Certainly women show greater understanding of other people (sometimes called 'empathy') and this is a valuable asset in many professions.[20] Combined with a general interest in promoting social bonds and fulfilment, it is not surprising that women are attracted to, and excel in, the helping professions such as teaching, nursing, counselling and personnel work (and some aspects of law and medicine). In such occupations they have contact with people in need, for whom they can provide support and guidance, a role which they usually find personally satisfying. Certain sales fields, such as life assurance (or 'personal financial planning' as it is euphemistically described) may come into this category because sensitivity to the needs of the client is a relevant skill. Research in the US has shown that women perform as well as men in a variety of sales positions, and an increasing proportion of women are moving into fields such as real estate and insurance.

A question addressed recently by Rosemary Lagace at the University of Kentucky is whether saleswomen would be more stress-prone than their male counterparts given all the conflicting demands placed upon them.[21] For example, clients seek to purchase at the lowest possible price, sales managers want high revenue, the production department wants a smooth flow of orders and no customer complaints, while family members demand that more time and attention be devoted to them. Obviously, trying to juggle all this can be stressful; so how do women respond by comparison with men?

Studying 90 saleswomen and 50 salesmen working for various US companies (mainly industrial), Lagace found hardly any difference on a variety of stress dimensions. The women showed a slightly greater tendency towards 'role overload', meaning that they rather felt pulled in too many different directions, but there were no differences on other stress measures, nor on overall job satisfaction or performance.

If women lack aggressiveness in the sales field, they apparently make up for it with other advantages such as verbal fluency and the management of personal relationships. According to some psychologists, women are better able to perceive selling as a social exchange process and to recognise their own interdependence in it. Men may be more likely to evoke resistance by adopting the 'hard sell' approach.

Patterns of Communication

Men and women frequently misunderstand each other because they have different patterns of communication. In fact, women often complain that their husbands don't communicate at all, while men complain that their wives 'nag' them when they just want to relax and read the newspaper.

What is not always understood is that men and women use talk for different reasons—men to promote dominance and action and women to express feelings and build social bonds. Women are three times as likely to make a telephone call when they have nothing special to say, with the result that a husband's anger over his wife's use of the telephone (not to mention teenage daughters) is quite normal. Women are annoyed by men interrupting them in an impatient, arrogant way and changing the topic (usually towards sport, sex or politics), but most of all they are annoyed by men's refusal to talk at all. Women ask three times as many questions as men, but apparently more out of a need to initiate and maintain conversation than desire for an answer.

New York researchers Sherman and Haas say that a standard husband-wife conversation runs like this: she states an emotional problem and a few seconds later he says 'Here's what you do ...' This makes her angry because she did not raise the issue seeking a solution. She wanted emotional support and a good listener, not instant advice.[22] Where women want 'grooming', men are usually trying to get things 'done'.

The apparent inability of men to express their feelings may have disadvantages. Some think it could be related to the male proneness to duodenal ulcers, heart disease and suicide, though there is no real evidence to support this idea. It is true that men suffer more following marital breakdown than do women. Perhaps this is because they miss their wife's social support, whereas the wife has little to lose in this respect—she never really got much emotional support in the first place. But of course, men often lose their children and homes as well as their wife upon divorce, (which happens less often to women) so the experience is more life-altering and traumatising to men.

Incidentally, my own work on marital dissatisfaction has shown that relationship difficulty is connected with styles of attempted influence.[23] Two types of women appeared as most discontented: the rampant feminist who engaged in direct confrontation with her partner and the very traditional woman who used emotional manipulation (e.g. crying and appeals to love and affection) as a means of getting her way. The happiest women were intermediate between these extremes, favouring 'give and take' negotiation in their relationships. This research needs reflecting so that the power styles of happy and unhappy men are investigated.

Apart from differences in use of conversation, men and women have different body language. Females use greater amounts of gaze, smiling and facial expressiveness than men, and usually tolerate greater physical proximity (both indications of a desire for intimacy). There are, however, some circumstances in which excessive gaze and touching become threatening to a woman and are likely to be viewed as 'harassment'. Men are also particularly sensitive about being touched or stared at by other men, since their usual orientation toward men is competitive.

There are other sex differences in the preferred use of space. For example, women feel more intimate when seated beside another person, whereas men tend to sit opposite a table from another person, without meaning to appear cold. Men emit more dominance signals than women, for example spreading their limbs wide so as to occupy more territory. (Women are at a particular disadvantage in wearing skirts, since if they are tight they cannot spread their legs, and if they could it would appear indecent.) Men shuffle about in their seat, showing more general restlessness than women (consistent with a general tendency to be active and 'get things done') and they emit more aggressive signals like clenching their fists.

Conclusion

In short, men and women are quite different in many respects, including talents, motivation, personality, and social communication, and these differences are largely innate. In many occupations men are almost certain to predominate, but women have several advantages over men that might help them to succeed in certain areas of the business world.

1 Women are more genuinely interested in the needs and problems of other people and hence come across as more warm and friendly, less pushy, manipulative and threatening. They thus simultaneously avoid two of the prime errors in sales and negotiation—indifference and the hard-sell.

2 Women are willing to spend more time getting to know a client and their life-style and are less obsessed with making immediate points about the virtues of a product they are selling.

3 Women's social intuition and linguistic skills provide them with greater sensitivity to the reactions of clients and greater verbal fluency. These attributes equip them particularly for jobs such as lawyer and counsellor.

4 Within a company women function as conciliators and provide a network of communication through which emotional strains and grievances can be aired and ameliorated. Hence they often operate informally as personnel officers and generally 'humanise' a work environment.

Thus women have an important role to play in the world of business and commerce, and one that is complementary rather than opposed to that of men.

Finally, we should not forget one of the central points that the women's movement has undoubtedly helped to establish over the last few decades—that whatever the average differences between men and women, there are enormous variations in ability and motivation within each sex and a great deal of overlap between them, so there is every reason, scientific, moral and economic, to treat people as individuals first and foremost—not as members of a vast, amorphous, gender group. Discrimination of any kind, whether based on traditional prejudices or attempts to correct perceived historical 'wrongs' (reverse discrimination), is likely to be counterproductive as well as unfair.

Notes

1 Kirkcaldy, B., 'Sex and Personality Differences in Occupational Interests', *Personality and Individual Differences*, **9**, 1988, pp. 7-13.

2 Report jointly commissioned by the National Association of Schoolmasters and Union of Women Teachers and the Engineering Council (see *The Times*, 10 May 1991, 'Girls Will Be Girls and Boys Will Be Boys', article by David Tytler, Education Editor).

3 Wilson, G., *The Great Sex Divide*, London: Peter Owen, 1989.

4 Benbow, C. and Stanley, J., 'Sex Differences in Mathematical Reasoning Ability: More Facts', *Science*, **222**, 1983, 2 December, pp. 1029-31.

5 Study by Dr Martin Hughes of Exeter University, reported in *The Times*, 11 September 1988.

6 Lynn, R., *The Secret of the Miracle Economy: Different National Attitudes to Competitiveness and Money*, London: The Social Affairs Unit, 1991.

7 *The Times Saturday Review*, 7 December 1991.

8 Ellis, L., 'Evidence of Neuroandrogenic Etiology of Sex Roles from a Combined Analysis of Human, Non-Human Primate and Non-Primate Mammalian Studies', *Personality and Individual Differences*, **7**, 1986, pp. 519-52.

9 Wilson, G., 'Finger Length as an Index of Assertiveness in Women', *Personality and Individual Differences*, **4**, 1983, pp. 111-12.

10 Eibl-Eibesfeldt, I., 'Dominance, Submission and Love: Sexual Pathologies from the Perspective of Ethology', In Feierman, J.R., (ed.), *Paedophilia: Biosocial Dimensions*, New York: Springer-Verlag, 1991.

11 *Daily Telegraph*, 2 April 1992.

12 Over, R., 'Research Productivity and Impact of Male and Female Psychologists', *American Psychologist*, **37**, 1982, pp. 24-31.

13 'Sex Discrimination in Universities', Report by Association of University Teachers, UK, Spring 1992.

14 Steffert, B., 'Sex Differences in Time Taken To Do a PhD', Paper delivered at British Psychology Society Annual Conference, 1991.

15 Levin, M., *Feminism and Freedom*, New Brunswick, NJ: Transaction Inc., 1987, p. 142.

16 Quoted in Wilson, G., *The Great Sex Divide, op. cit.*, p. 140.

17 Cowan, N. and Davidson, G., 'Salient Childhood Memories', *Journal of Genetic Psychology*, 145, 1984, pp. 101-7.

18 Goldberg, S. and Lewis, M., 'Play Behaviour in the Year-Old Infant: Early Sex Differences', *Child Development*, 40, 1969, pp. 21-31.

19 Hall, J., 'Gender Effects in Decoding Non-Verbal Cues', *Psychological Bulletin*, **85**, 1978, pp. 845-57.

20 Gilligan, C., *In a Different Voice*, Cambridge MA: Harvard University Press, 1982.

21 Lagace, R., 'Role-Stress Differences Between Salesmen and Saleswomen: Effect on Job Satisfaction and Performance', *Psychological Reports*, **62**, 1988, pp. 815-25.

22 'Big Thoughts About Small Talk', *Time*, 17 September 1984.

23 Wilson, G., 'Feminism and Marital Dissatisfaction', *Personality and Individual Differences*, **2**, 1981, pp. 343-46.

Children and Feminism

Michael Levin

Logic textbooks commonly warn against the Fallacy of Composition, the inference that what is true of the parts of a whole must be true of the whole. If you think that a wall weighs ten pounds because each of its bricks do, or that the ocean cannot be blue because water drops are colourless, this is your error.

That much confusion is pretty rare. Most bad reasoning is transparent when made explicit, and, to judge by textbook examples, unlikely to fool anyone. Bad reasoning is harder to spot in the wild, however, with no authorial guide at hand and fallacy-mongers taking no pains to be clear. And as it happens John Stuart Mill once did commit the fallacy of composition in anger, in a most instructive form. Mill, a utilitarian, proposed a proof of sorts that the *summum bonum* is 'the greatest happiness of the greatest number'. He argued, first, that the only test of whether something is good is that people actually want it, and went on: 'each person's happiness is a good to that person, and the general happiness, therefore, a good to the aggregate of all persons'. (*Utilitarianism*, pt. II.) The 'therefore' is unearned. That each person wants his *own* happiness is no reason whatever to think that anyone wants the happiness of all; if anything it is a reason to the contrary. If *A* wants *A* to be happy and *B* wants *B* to be happy, neither cares whether both *A* and *B* are happy. Nor can 'the aggregate of all persons' desire the general happiness, since aggregates of people are not themselves sentient beings with desires. The pair consisting of *A* and *B* has no desires of its own. So Mill has produced nothing that desires the general happiness, thereby failing on his own grounds to show that the general happiness is a good.

Mill may have had in mind that, while no one cares about the happiness of all as a whole, each bit of it—the happiness of each particular person—matters to someone or other, so that the happiness of all and what really matters, individual happiness, rise and fall together. But the situation is more complex, since, as economists say, utilities are not linearly independent. A and B might each be able to achieve 30 units of utility were the other not around, but only 20 units apiece when pursuing utility at the same time. Indeed, B might be able to achieve 25 units, if he must act at the same time as A, were A limited to 17. In that case, maximizing overall utility means reducing A's. Worse still, if A's next unit of effort would produce more utility if exerted for B than for himself—as can happen if A is much better off than B—maximizing requires A to work for B. Maximizing *must* have such consequences, given that only individuals can be happy. Working for the happiness of all means working for the happiness of somebody—somebody you care about, or somebody you do not.

The real-world compromise reached in western society is the pursuit by each individual of his own well-being in accordance with rules that let everyone else do likewise. These rules include respect for property rights, non-aggression, co-operation, and responsibility for one's own acts. The good life is thought to consist in conforming to these rules, not in contributing to a meaningless aggregate.

Who's Whose?

Having warmed up on Mill, let us turn to some slogans, advertisements and editorials. Just today the present author saw a bumper sticker intended to protest military spending: 'Do We Fear Our Enemies More than We Love Our Kids?' The Children's Defense Fund, an influential lobby in the US, has (together with the 'Robin Hood Foundation') run a series of advertisements asking 'Does America Love its Children?' According to the Children's Defense Fund, America most certainly does not. 'The mightiest nation in the world is about to be done in, by its own children. How, you ask? By their continued neglect.' In response to a series of shootings in slum schools, the *New York Times* published an editorial entitled 'Mowing Down Our Children.' Citing the large number of illegitimate children living in poverty, an essay entitled 'Our Children, Our Future' in *Columbia* Magazine found:

> our society becoming increasingly selfish and stressful, and less

willing to care about children. Perhaps instead of debating 'family values' we should start to value families, recognizing that rearing children is the most challenging job in society, and that the quality of our collective future depends upon it being done well.[1]

Naturally, the *Times*, *Columbia* and the Children's Defense Fund teem with ideas for saving our children, most requiring forced income redistribution and few involving parental care as normally understood. But prior to any discussion of these ideas, or why they are urged in just these terms at just this time, I call your attention to a point of logic. *All the items mentioned*—and more could be cited without limit—*commit the fallacy of composition, and all commit it in more or less the form Mill did.* In fact, the main difference is that Mill seems to have been genuinely confused, whereas the Children's Defense Fund *et al* evidently know just what they are doing.

The bumper sticker question, for instance, is quite subtle. Since parental affection is a stronger, more immediate feeling than worry about threats, one first response is to agree that, yes, we do love our kids more than we fear our enemies. One can then be manipulated—into agreeing, for instance, that money for anti-terrorist measures should go to education. But pronouns are being used ambiguously. 'We' love 'our' kids one by one: I like my kids more than I fear terrorists and you like your kids more than you fear terrorists. The 'our' in 'our enemies' is collective, however, referring to the country as a whole. When usage is made consistent, so that the 'our' in 'our children' also refers to the country as a whole, the bumper sticker ceases to be persuasive. You like your kids more than you fear terrorists, but you may not like *mine* more. You might approve shifting all anti-terrorist funds to your own children's education, but shifting the anti-terrorist budget to 'our' children means a little more for yours, a little more for mine, and the rest for kids you don't know. The proposed shift may give the children *you* love too little to offset the increased risk to you (and them) attending military weakness. The best answer to the bumper sticker is 'Yes, I love *my* children more than I fear the common enemy, but not *all* children.'

Are Neglected Children 'Our' Problem?

Take the charge that 'America' is neglecting 'its' children, brought by the Children's Defense Fund on the grounds that '5.5 million American children do not regularly get enough to eat,' 'the US ranks 16th' in immunizing infants against polio, and '2.5 million American children were reported abused or neglected in the last year.' (I quote this from advertisements.) To be sure, these supposed facts are questionable. Children in the US below the poverty line actually consume a bit *more* protein daily than children above it, and as many vitamins and nutrients, for instance.[2] But more important than rectifying the facts is clarity about who precisely is neglecting whom. *I* certainly do not neglect or abuse my children, nor do I abuse any others. Those 2.5 million, assuming the figure reliable, are neglected by their own parents. Indeed, even 'children's advocates' admit that poor children go unvaccinated largely because their—usually unmarried—mothers do not take advantage of extant free immunization programmes. One shameless apologist cites 'long lines at the public clinics' as a 'barrier'.[3] Underfed, sickly children would signify *my* negligence only if I had some prior obligation to care for them, which I do not. These children are 'mine' only in being citizens of the same country I am. They are not mine, but their biological parents', in the sense of possession necessary for responsibility.

The idea that 'we as a society' (in the current cant phrase) should care for all children is pure fallacious Mill, but in fairness there is some bastardised Kant here too. A large philosophical literature has grown up around the right of each person to 'equal dignity'. Motivated in good part by its prospective application to children, a supposed deduction from this right is an obligation on others to see that everyone has the means to a dignified life.[4] However, Kantian respect for human dignity imposes only a duty not to coerce, manipulate or deceive others, not a duty to support them. Indeed, the clearest case imaginable of the use of people as means is viewing the more able as a resource for the less able. No doubt all children should be treated with 'equal respect', and equity—the principle that like cases should be treated alike—implies that all children should be treated as well as mine should be. But other children will be treated as well as mine if *their* fathers treat them as well as I treat mine, not if *I* treat them as well.

Just as pursuing the 'general' good means asking some people to work for others, keeping 'our children from falling behind' (The Children's Defense Fund again) means, in practice, and in most cases, government redirection of resources from more to less responsible adults. The most familiar such redistributive effort in the US is Head Start, which spends several billion dollars annually enriching pre-school environments for poor children in a so-far futile effort to improve their academic performance.[5] The Clinton administration, enthusiastically agreeing that childhood disease is 'our' problem, not a problem for the children of neglectful parents, intends to buy up all the vaccine in the US to inoculate children free, and to hire nurses to find children whose parents do not seek out inoculation. Of course, these vaccinations will be 'free' only in a Pickwickian sense. Their projected annual cost of £800 million is to be borne by the taxpayer, a little more of whose labour is then going to support the children of negligent strangers.

The economic problems with such state intervention are familiar. Legally commandeering drugs at below-market rates—ironically, paying market rates would be called 'enriching the drug companies with taxpayer's money'—makes it harder for drug manufacturers to stay in business, and impossible for the drug manufacturers who do survive to be sure of recovering the costs of developing new drugs. The result: fewer drugs.

At the moral level, talk of 'our' children begs the basic question: what right has anyone to force A to support B's children? Having children is voluntary; those who can't afford children can refrain from having them. Even liberationists shy away from claiming for the irresponsible a right to have children, preferring to call children inevitable. What seems most clear is a right to direct one's resources to one's own offspring. It is often replied that no-one will care for neglected children unless 'we' do. Logically, it suffices to point out that obligations end at not causing harm, and no-one but their parents are harming these children. Indeed, bringing a child into being cannot literally worsen (or better) its situation, but those who create a child are commonly thought to harm it if they do not provide for it above some minimum. Although those who had no part in creating a child may well have a duty to force the parents to support it, they do not themselves harm it if they do not support it. The child is no worse off than he would have been if these indifferent adults did not exist.

In practice these reminders do not stop 'children's advocates' from displaying neglected children to generate guilt. In other words, words I use with intent, 'children's advocates' use these children as human shields for the purpose of moral blackmail. For blackmail is nothing else than an offer to sell forbearance from a wrongful act, and a human shield is anyone whose suffering a blackmailer advertises to promote his sale. Hostages, we might add, are the potential victims of the wrong whose omission is on sale. And, in promising to lift unmerited guilt about babies of irresponsible mothers and absent fathers if we socialise parenthood, 'children's advocates' also encourage the parents to use their own children as human shields. This moral blackmail turns into extortion—blackmail holding the buyer hostage with threats of violence—with warnings that today's underprivileged child is tomorrow's criminal preying on the society that neglected him.

Blackmail and extortion are evil in themselves, and yielding to them always encourages more, in this case in the form of more shield-children. Continued assumption of care for neglected children and their mothers signals that there is no need to worry about the consequences of producing babies so long as the babies are presented as *faits accompli*. Eventually, the cost of appeasement becomes insupportable. An expert is cited in *Columbia* as recommending 'family-related income support through the tax system' so that 'single mothers [can] have some time at home ... without having to turn to a stigmatized and inadequate welfare program.' One would have thought that preventing illegitimacy by stigmatizing it was a major function of sexual morality.

Feminism and Children

The case against nationalized parenthood is understood by everyone but academics and the governments they advise; what is new is the push for it in *faux* Millsian language. I suggest that this innovation is a rhetorical change adopted by feminists to allay the distrust of feminism that most people continue to feel. The feminist goal of disrupting the 'patriarchal' family, separating mothers from babies in the name of liberation, has always seemed profoundly adverse to children. Feminists have learned to advocate the same goal, by the same means, in a more child-friendly vocabulary.

Feminists always sound anti-child. As much as anything, what at first titillated the media about feminists, making them 'hot' items, was their breathtakingly vulgar fulmination against marriage, sexual intercourse, and motherhood. Here are some early samples:

> There are several more or less standard pieces of armament used in [the] assault upon wives, but the biggest one is generally the threat of force ... To take as an example [the wife] may be tired and feel insulted by her husband's belching and farting at the table. Can you imagine her husband's fury if it got back to him that she told someone he farted at the table?[6]

> I think it's wonderful that women have discovered masturbation, because it will enable women to keep apart from men as long as necessary ... Some of the women I know are so pathetic. They run around looking for a man, any man, just because they don't know how to masturbate.[7]

Far from having mellowed, many feminists today sound as if they have gone completely round the twist:

> Dirty words stay dirty because they express a hate for women as inferiors ... a hate for women's genitals, a hate for women's bodies, a hate for the insides of women ... the penis itself signif[ies] power over women ...[8]

Such outbursts cause public relations problems, which Betty Friedan fretted about as early as 1981 in *The Second Stage*.[9] Ordinary people resent this almost antinomian hatred of so much that they prize. They sense that the logical conclusion of feminists' anti-natal, pro-lesbian sentiments is the end of the human race (a prospect some 'ecofeminists' come near to embracing). Their everyday experience contradicts the dogma that sex differences are bias artifacts. That is why, despite their skill at badgering them into assenting to platitudes about equal opportunity, average people dislike feminists.

Backlash!

So it was not altogether a surprise when, in the early 1990s, the media discovered a 'backlash' against feminism. Susan Faludi wrote a book of that name,[10] and, with Gloria Steinem, duly appeared on the cover of *Time*. There was much tut-tuttery on the talk shows. To be sure, the terms in which the debate was conducted made all the heavy breathing seem unnecessary. The principal thesis of *Backlash*, media bias against feminism, was refuted by the media's own adulation of the book. My wife, a target of *Backlash*, was invited to debate Miss Faludi on TV, and then asked by the producers to sit offscreen because Miss Faludi feared 'contentiousness'. (This concession was remarkable for American TV, which thrives on confrontation.) I may be prejudiced, being another target of *Backlash*, but *I* have never graced the cover of a national magazine, nor am I, like Gloria Steinem, famous for being well-known. If my wife and I are among the threats to feminism, it is safe as houses. Probably the first that most people heard of the backlash was that it had been foiled.

Yet, as I say, at a deeper level feminists were right to worry—not about media conspiracies or a few academic critics, but about reality. Things were just not working out as feminists said they would. After all, the main exhibit of Susan Faludi's case was media interest in a 1986 Harvard–Yale study showing that the chances of first-time marriage for women decline sharply with age;[11] the study was never published. (My own impression at the time was of no more than modest media interest in it.) Miss Faludi gamely attacks the study itself—with scant success, since of mathematical necessity no fewer women marry for the first time after age n than after $n+m$; if the Harvard–Yale study has a fault it is that of proving the obvious. Yet the crucial question Miss Faludi avoids is why the study, which on its face is not concerned with feminism at all, was so widely seen as damaging to it. The reason, clearly, was the universal recognition that women wish to marry, and the equally universal hunch that feminist prescriptions war with marriage. (The study also supports the despised 'stereotype' that male attraction to youth has deeper roots than 'sexist conditioning'.) Explicitly, demographers were saying that a woman who postpones marriage risks never being married; implicitly, they were saying that a woman who leads a liberated life, deferring marriage to pursue the feminist ideal of fulfilment, risks never being married. (Both Susan Faludi and Gloria Steinem are unmarried and have no children.) Since women do value marriage very highly, demographers were suggesting that the feminist ideal is a bad one. It begs the question to call the Harvard-Yale study an attempt to stampede young women into marriage, since women would not panic unless they already considered marriage highly desirable.

It is strange that Miss Faludi keeps insisting that her basic hope is to see 'women's independence [of] domesticity, family and motherhood'.[12] From this insistence one would expect to find her pleased that feminist life choices reduce the chance of such dependency, rather than at pains to prove that they do not. 'Marriage is terrible', she says, in effect, 'and how dare you accuse me of undermining it?' This response is of a piece with the feminist response to accusations of lesbianism: 'There is absolutely nothing wrong with being a lesbian and how dare you call me one.' Incidentally, Miss Faludi is more consistent, and on firmer factual grounds, about divorce. One would expect her to minimise the adverse effects of divorce, another corollary of 'independence', and she does. Another study that appeared in the mid-1980s claimed a 73 per cent drop in women's standard of living accompanies divorce, and Miss Faludi replies, correctly, that the true figure is closer to 33 per cent.[13] (The media spin put on this study was not that feminist nostrums, by encouraging divorce, harm women, but that divorce is another occasion for 'society' to discriminate.) Yet her victory is Pyrrhic: if divorce reduces a women's income by 'only' one-third, much more such liberation and women will be lost.

Being Pro-Family, Feminist Style

Limited as their grasp of the 'backlash' was, feminists realised that they had better confirm their bona fides as members of the human race. But they faced a dilemma. What might be called the thesis was their determination to show themselves 'for' families and children. The antithesis, or antitheses, were the notions they wished to retain while doing so: that sex roles are artifacts, that drastically de-emphasising motherhood is necessary for liberation, that freedom is slavery—i.e. that women are so brainwashed they will choose domestic roles unless prevented. The synthesis was a new-found avidity for 'our' children. The 'children' bit showed that feminists were not as demented as they often gave evidence of being, while the 'our' bit, as explained, ensured continued state involvement.

A case study in this dialectic is Sara Ruddick's widely praised paean to 'maternal devotion', 'or the capacity for attentive love'.[14] Shaped by the mother's interest in 'the preservation, growth and [social] acceptability' of her child, this capacity makes mothers humble, resilient, good-humoured, empathic and selfless,[15] points repeated at considerable length. One might at first welcome Professor Ruddick's work as a needed if laboured restatement of the obvious, but that would be a mistake. For one thing, she denies that maternity and maternal devotion are in any way innate; '"maternal" is a social category,' she declares. For another, she holds that maternal care has been distorted by the 'dominant' society, which is 'middle-class, white, Protestant, capitalist, patriarchal' and centred around 'the heterosexual nuclear family'.[16] As a result, 'maternal thought will have to be transformed by feminist consciousness,' which means 'assimilating men into childcare both inside and outside the home,' and establishing 'good day-care centers with flexible hours ... to which parents could trust their children from infancy on':

> [W]e must work to bring a *transformed* maternal thought in the public realm, to make the preservation and growth of *all* children a work of public conscience and legislation ... the generalization of attentive love to *all* children requires politics.[17]

This position differs from that of previous feminists only in being less coherent. For surely, if Professor Ruddick really thinks maternal love is as wonderful as she says she does, the last thing she should want to see is infants being cared for by strangers. She would want to see women having and rearing lots of babies, not the separation of mothers and babies 'from infancy on' in accordance with 'politics'.

This doublethink (or deceptiveness) crops up repeatedly. In the same breath with which feminists express support for the family, they make it clear that the families they support are to be 'diverse'. These diverse families include unmarried mothers, cohabiting couples, homosexual couples, working parents plus nanny, step-parents with step-children ... As for the unwaged mother living with one husband all her life, feminists announce the passing of *that* family with evident satisfaction. Yet it is a family of just this sort—not an unmarried mother with illegitimate children, not a household of homosexuals—that everyone wants to belong to and most certainly wishes for his children. Feminist support for the family as most people understand it is hard to tell from opposition.

For readers not fully conversant with feminist terms of art, the conventional family is called the 'Ozzie and Harriet model', after a 1950s American TV show in which Ozzie and Harriet Nelson and their sons Ricky and David essentially played themselves. Harriet always had cookies ready when the boys, dressed in nondescript slacks and open-neck white shirts, came home from school. Family problems concerned grades, dating, after-school jobs and, in later years, Ricky's budding singing career as a sort of sanitized Elvis. Whatever the Nelson's private life may have been like, the life they represented is the one most people want. For this, as James Q. Wilson has said, they are 'the most maligned figures in the history of television ... regarded by the eminences of the media and the academy as cartoon[s], fit only for ridicule and rejection'.[18] Such is the attitude of pro-family feminists.

The Real Backlash

The causal significance of social phenomena, especially belief systems like feminism, is hard to sort out. Feminism is certainly responsible for discrimination against men, but other correlates of feminism might be further effects, or causes of feminism (which feminism rationalises, perhaps), or effects along with feminism of underlying factors. Nonetheless, feminism has become associated with a number of social changes over the past thirty years, including the widespread employment outside the home of mothers of young children, a reduction in time spent with children by mothers, and marital instability. These associations are based partly on causal common sense: belligerent I-have-a-right-to-be-my-own-person declarations seem bound to displease husbands, for instance. But in addition, feminism is implicated in these changes because it is seen as *endorsing* them. By their hostility to traditional marriage and motherhood, feminists committed themselves to the alternatives, which, outside the delusional realm of feminist utopia, are— when not childlessness—single motherhood, cohabitation, divorce, day-care, and full-time employment outside the home. And because of these well-earned associations, the real backlash against feminism is coming from social scientists, who have reluctantly concluded that every one of these changes is, by ordinary standards, bad.

For when scientists like Victor Fuchs and Diane Riklis announce in a lead article in a major journal that 'American children are in trouble', and correction is made for the fallacy of composition, they are really saying that the children of liberation are in trouble:

> Cultural changes, such as the growing incidence of divorce and unwed motherhood, reduce the income available to children ... [T]he jump in the proportion of married women with one child or more under age six who are in the labor force probably resulted in some decrease in home-cooked meals, help with homework, and other nonmarket goods and services since 1960.[19]

The authors estimate that, principally because of mothers holding paid jobs, parents spent 10 fewer hours per week with their children in 1986 than in 1960.[20] And social scientists no longer endorse the shibboleth that these fewer hours are qualitatively superior because Mom feels more fulfilled. The fact is that, in the US, every indicator of youthful deviance has risen since 1965: juvenile violent crime rates have quadrupled, the teenage suicide rate has tripled, scores on standardised tests of scholastic aptitude have dropped almost a standard deviation, and television watching has increased by 40 per cent.[21] Barbara Whitehead writes even more starkly:

> Nationally, more than 70 per cent of all juveniles in state reform institutions come from fatherless homes ... Family diversity in the form of increasing numbers of single-parent and step-parent families does not strengthen the social fabric. It dramatically weakens and undermines society, placing new burdens on schools, courts, prisons, and the welfare system. These new families are not an improvement on the nuclear family, nor are they even just as good, whether you look at outcomes for children or outcomes for society as a whole.[22]

One irony in the emphasis on paid employment for women is that recent inquiry has confirmed the conjecture made in an earlier essay that, for mothers, working is essentially running in place.[23] One case study found that childcare consumed 80 per cent of the after-tax income of a working mother of three.[24] If a single income no longer suffices for a middle-class standard of living, as feminists are so eager to insist, the stark choice facing the middle class is fewer children or finding the means to lower living costs in relation to income. (Drastically reducing taxation for social spending is one obvious means.)

Reluctance to Challenge Feminism

Miss Whitehead also explains the reluctance of social scientists to publicise these findings: 'Some are fearful that they will be attacked by feminist colleagues, or, more generally, that their comments will be regarded as an effort to turn back the clock to the 1950s'. In other words, whatever feminism may have originally contributed to the present malaise, it now exercises a veto over solutions. Because many people assume that feminism is on the side of virtue, no solution is countenanced unless conformable to it. Since feminists are dead against the obvious—making divorce harder, re-stigmatizing illegitimacy, searching for ways to allow women to stay home, and reinforcing sex roles which would all 'turn back the clock'— confusion and irresolution continue. Consider the palpable failure of nerve in a recent essay, 'The Crisis of the Kids'. After repeating Miss Whitehead's points—that 'Career and self-fulfilment have got ahead of caring responsibility', that divorce and illegitimacy correlate strongly with poverty, crime and drug use, that quality time is a 'delusion'—the author immediately takes cover:

> The emphasis on the importance of the family should not be read as an attack on single mothers or their children. Nor does an emphasis on the value of the family imply that what we require is a reassertion of male authority or a reduction of the hard-earned rights of women.[25]

But of course it *does*—if not an 'attack' (for who would 'attack' rights?), then certainly a reassessment of the current de-emphasis on motherhood. Lacking the heart to challenge feminism, the essay concludes by blaming television for the inability of parents to bring up their children properly.

Lessons for Britain

Britain can avoid the American precedent. It is certainly way behind the US: Britain's juvenile homicide rate is perhaps one-twentieth of America's, for instance. A very important difference, I believe, is the greater seriousness of the American race problem and the alliance in the US of the forces of 'anti-racism' and 'anti-sexism'. Bear in mind that almost 70 per cent of the live births to American blacks are now illegitimate, and that the divorce rate among American blacks is 67 per cent. (As might be expected, black levels of antisocial behaviour are astronomical: 25 per cent of black males are in prison at some point in their lives.) But precisely because for all practical purposes the black family no longer exists, any criticism of illegitimacy and marital instability, any suggestion that Ozzie and Harriet families are not so bad, is attacked as implicitly critical of blacks. Potential critics often censor themselves once they realise this implication. It would be useful if, in Britain, feminists were not allowed to make common cause so easily with racial radicals.

The irony in this alliance of feminism and racial radicalism is that, while feminists and traditionalists agree about very little, they should be at one in deploring the attitude of American black men toward women in the US. It is not simply the apparent readiness of black men to view women as 'sex objects'. It is, rather, the pervasiveness of violence in black personal relations. That feminists should find themselves criticising the critics of such behaviour, thereby in effect defending it, shows how fatally they are drawn to any anti-social force. To the extent that people are willing to reassert the value of the societies they construct, 'backlash' is inevitable.

Notes

1 Aron, L., `Our Children, Our Future', *Columbia*, Fall, 1992, p. 42.

2 *Nutrition Monitoring in the United States: A Report from the Nutrition Monitoring Evaluation Committee*, US Department of Agriculture, Washington DC: Government Printing Office, July 1986.

3 Pearson, H.A., President of the American Academy of Paediatrics, cited in Hilts, P., 'Drug Companies Warn Administration Against Vaccine Program', *New York Times*, April 2 1993, p. A20.

4 See e.g. Kagan, S., *The Limits of Morality*, Oxford: Oxford University Press, 1989.

5 Head Start began in the 1960s on the assumption that low grades are caused by poor environments. When Head Start children turned out to perform no better than controls three years after leaving the programme, (Spitz, H., *The Raising of Intelligence*, Hillsdale, NJ: Erlbaum, 1986, pp. 81-94) follow-up programmes began. When the

follow-ups also proved ineffective (*ibid.*), the rationale for Head Start shifted to its beneficial effects on social behaviour (see e.g. Zigler, E. and Berman, W., 'Discerning the Future of Childhood Intervention', *American Psychologist*, 38, 1983). These beneficial effects have proven ephemeral in turn, yet the Clinton Administration plans to expand Head Start. The latest justification has not been announced.

6 Jones, B., 'The Dynamics of Marriage and Motherhood', in Morgan, R., (ed.), *Sisterhood is Powerful*, NY: Vintage, 1970, p. 46f.

7 Seaman, B., *Free and Female*, NY: Fawcett, 1972, p. 69.

8 Dworkin, A., *Intercourse*, NY: The Free Press, 1987, pp. 170-73.

9 New York: Simon & Schuster.

10 *Backlash*, NY: Simon & Schuster, 1992.

11 *Op. cit.*, pp. 9-14.

12 E.g. *op. cit.*, p. 117.

13 The original study was Weitzman, L., *The Divorce Revolution*, NY: The Free Press, 1985; for more accurate numbers, see Whitehead, B.D., 'Dan Quayle was Right', *The Atlantic Monthly*, May 1993, p. 62.

14 'Maternal Thinking' in Pearsall, M. (ed.), *Women and Values*, Belmont CA: Wadsworth, 1986, pp. 340-51; also see *Maternal Thinking*, Boston, Mass: Beacon, 1989.

15 *Op. cit.*, p. 348.

16 *Op. cit.*, p. 341.

17 *Op. cit.*, pp. 349-50.

18 'The Family-Values Debate', *Commentary*, April 1993, p. 31.

19 'America's Children: Economic Perspectives and Policy Options', *Science*, 22, 3 January 1992, pp. 41-46. The authors favour 'a general redistribution from higher to lower income,' but reject employer-mandated programmes because so few poor children live in households where anyone works!

20 *Ibid.*, p. 44.

21 See Bennett, W., *Index of Leading Cultural Indicators I*, Washington, DC: The Heritage Foundation, 1993.

22 Whitehead, B.D., *op. cit.*

23 Levin, M., 'Women, Work, Biology and Justice', in Quest, C., (ed.), *Equal Opportunities: A Feminist Fallacy*, London: IEA Health and Welfare Unit, 1992.

24 'Economics Puts a Mother's Career on Hold', *The New York Times*, 30 January 1993.

25 Zucherman, M., 'The Crisis of the Kids', *US News and World Report*, 12 April 1993.

Why Aren't All Women Feminists?

Joan Kennedy Taylor

There is a general assumption, which is probably true, that the average woman in the US and Britain doesn't react very positively to the word feminism, however she defines it. Margaret Forster in her 1984 book, *Significant Sisters*, wrote in her introduction that one of the riddles of feminism is 'why it has not attracted an enormous rank-and-file following among women themselves, why it is still as necessary as it was in the nineteenth century to ask a woman if she *is* a feminist'. The plain truth, she went on, 'is that not only do large numbers of women feel apathetic but many more actively hate feminism'.[1]

All feminists agree that women have suffered and do suffer legal and social disadvantages when compared to men—they differ on what to do about it, and their efforts are often opposed by non-feminist women. In the US, supporters of the Equal Rights Amendment found to their surprise during the campaign for ratification in the 1970s and 1980s that legislators in state after state heard from a substantial number of women who declared themselves opposed to feminism and who were very suspicious of the idea of equality before the law, apparently fearing that it would deprive them of their husbands' economic support and physical protection.

Since most women will admit in private conversation that they know that they are sometimes treated in ways to which they object—on the job, in the street, at home, or when engaging in business transactions—purely because of their gender, why do their feminist champions have such a bad reputation?

The Perception of Feminism

In a 1980 book, *The Sceptical Feminist*, Janet Radcliffe Richards devoted her concluding chapter to the fact that feminism (which she defines as the acceptance of the proposition 'that women suffer from systematic social injustice because of their sex')[2] is an unpopular movement, partly because 'feminism, by its very nature, is a thing which it is extremely difficult to get across'.[3] The acceptance of things the way they are, she thinks, is so deeply ingrained in people that it is genuinely hard for them to see those things that are unjust about the status quo. But she says, further, people see feminism as *unattractive*, both because its proponents appear strident and because 'since people's wishes have been formed in a background of tradition, feminism cannot help opposing many of those wishes'.

> The traditional ideas of romance, which depend on keeping men and women in their relative positions of power and dependence, still preoccupy at least nine-tenths of the population. Most women still dream about beauty, dress, weddings, dashing lovers, domesticity and babies; most men still aspire to success with beautiful women, relationships in which they are dominant, and a home in which their slippers are warmed and their wishes given priority over everything else. There may not be much hope, for most people, of fulfilling these wishes in their entirety, but if feminists seem (as they do) to want to eliminate nearly all of these things—beauty, sex conventions, families and all—for most people that simply means the removal of everything in life which is worth living for.[4]

This reaction is not new. It is often hard to imagine what life would be like if the social structure we have known from infancy were to change in some respect. In fact, without tradition and custom we would have little sense of security. When John Stuart Mill's *The Subjection of Women* was published in 1869, he pointed out this fact when he acknowledged that it would be difficult for his readers to accept his arguments.

> [T]ruly the understandings of the majority of mankind would need to be much better cultivated than has ever yet been the case, before they can be asked to place such reliance in their own power of estimating arguments, as to give up practical principles in which they have been born and bred and which are the basis of much of the existing order of the world, at the first argumentative attack which they are not capable of logically resisting.[5]

Since everyone grows up with certain assumptions about male and female roles that are based on custom, the effects of feminism have been most generally appreciated in retrospect, after change has occurred. No one would disagree today with the statement that the nineteenth-century feminists were absolutely correct in their protests against the common-law status of married women with respect to contracts, property, and the guardianship of children. Similarly now it seems inconceivable to British and American citizens that women should not have the vote, and the suffragettes who were vilified and force-fed by the police in their own day are acclaimed as having performed a great service to humanity. And we can no longer imagine our society without colleges and universities that admit women. But during the nineteenth century there was a long history of debate and concern over just such issues, calling into question the legal, religious, and social privileges that men enjoyed, and demanding that women be freed from subordination.

The impetus that we call feminism traces back to the publication of a number of classical liberal demands for women's equality in Western Europe in the 1790s (the best known of which today is Mary Wollstonecraft's 1792 *A Vindication of the Rights of Woman*). But what we generally mean when we speak of feminism today—and what is still controversial—is the movement that revived that impetus in the late sixties and early seventies.

Apart from the perception of feminism as threatening, what sort of an impact has this contemporary movement had on women in general?

Major Changes in Women's Lives

An American feminist, Bonnie Charles Bluh, listed some of the conditions she found in Ireland and England in 1971.[6] In both countries, fathers had many more rights over their children than mothers did. The father was the legal guardian, with the sole right to decide on their education, religion, and domicile; the father was the only one who could consent to an operation on a child; the father could take a child abroad without the consent of the mother, but she could not do likewise; a father could draw on a child's savings but a mother could not. Also, in both countries women had to reveal their income and tax forms to their husbands, but men were under no compulsion to reciprocate. A woman had to get her husband's permission for a number of actions: in Ireland, to get a passport, for almost any kind of financial arrangement or for any gynaecological operation; in England, to change her name or to obtain an inter-uterine device. In England, divorce, contraception, and abortion were legal; in Ireland there was no divorce even for non-Catholics, a woman member of parliament was not allowed by the Senate even to read a proposed bill to legalise contraception, and of course there was no abortion. In both countries, there were few women in upper echelon jobs; Ireland required women in the civil service to retire if they married; England had the same requirement for the diplomatic services. Women did not serve on juries in Ireland, and married women generally did not in England because of a requirement that a juror be a 'householder'—the husband was usually the householder of record.

The feminist movement in Ireland and England was in its infancy when Bonnie Bluh was travelling, and it could trace its inception to a meeting in Dublin in March 1971 and to four incidents in London that occurred between 1969 and 1971, a time when such laws and practices were routine. Some of these restrictions are still in effect; in the US today, some twenty-odd years later, most of them are not and seem unfair and antiquated. But at the time, to most people they were a matter of course.

Questioning legal inequalities caused many changes in society, but even larger changes had begun to occur in society as part of a revolution in expectations that might be viewed as a Hayekian spontaneous order. In the US, before there was any official feminist activity at all, a book by Betty Friedan, *The Feminist Mystique*,[7] had caused an enormous uproar. It questioned the way that American men and women had realised their dream of domesticity and pointed out compellingly that a large number of American housewives were unhappy. What were they doing? What all the experts told them to do—devoting themselves to marriage and family.

By the end of the nineteen-fifties, the average marriage age of

90

women in America dropped to 20, and was still dropping, into the teens. Fourteen million girls were engaged by 17. The proportion of women attending college in comparison with men dropped from 47 per cent in 1920 to 35 per cent in 1958. A century earlier, women had fought for higher education; now girls went to college to get a husband. By the mid-fifties, 60 per cent dropped out of college to marry, or because they were afraid too much education would be a marriage bar ... Then American girls began getting married in high school. And the women's magazines, deploring the unhappy statistics about these young marriages, urged that courses on marriage, and marriage counsellors, be installed in the high schools.[8]

By the late fifties and early sixties, magazines were reporting that the American housewife felt dissatisfied and trapped; that women were going to doctors in increasing numbers with unspecified tiredness and unspecified 'neurotic' problems of adjustment to life. Friedan called it 'the problem that has no name', and said it was because women had accepted a 'feminine mystique' that required them to spend their lives in service to others, with no outside interests of their own.

Paid Employment

The book was a bombshell. It became clear that a large number of women responded to Friedan's message, and a social revolution took place. Women started going back to school and taking entry level jobs for minuscule pay—not to abandon their husbands and children but to augment the lives they were living.

> The exodus of women from the home changed the face of American society. In an astonishingly short period of time, we became a society that asks women, 'What do you do?' before asking 'Are you married?' In 1960 only 19 per cent of American married women with children were in the labor force. By 1970 the figure was 28 per cent. By 1986, not only was a majority of women with children in the labor force, but a majority with children as young as one year old; the percentage of all American women in paid employment rose from 35 per cent in 1960 to 55 per cent in 1986.[9]

A writer for the *Boston Globe* reported in 1983, 'As recently as 1968, 62 per cent of women aged 14 to 22 told researchers at Ohio State University they expected to be housewives at age 35. By 1979, just 20 per cent of young women said they intended to be full-time homemakers.'[10] In 1983 also, a survey of 8,000 women in seven universities found only two who said they 'plan to be full-time homemakers.'[11]

What caused such a rapid change? It was influenced, after *The Feminine Mystique*, by other books that swiftly appeared, feminist analyses of society and books aimed directly at the exiting housewives, like a 1972 book, *How to Go to Work When Your Husband Is Against It, Your Children Aren't Old Enough and There's Nothing You Can Do Anyhow*.[12] The women who were changing their lives were also helped to do so by a feminist invention: consciousness raising. American feminists who came from the New Left invented this group experience, hoping to radicalise the women that came together to examine their lives. But the leaderless groups could not be controlled, and soon consciousness raising became a grassroots experience. By 1972, the National organization for Women (NOW) had as a primary activity the establishment of such groups, and brought over 100,000 women together within a year. Magazines like *Ms* published directions for setting up such groups, and groups formed among middle-class and blue-collar wives; even in high schools.

It was feminism that challenged the belief that the optimal destiny of every woman was to be a wife and mother. It was feminism that knocked down the barriers that kept women out of medical school, law school, and business school, and brought women an almost equal participation with men in the professions. Businesses caught on soon and provided the economic opportunity for women; feminism, whether acknowledged or not, provided the intellectual impetus for women to take advantage of those opportunities.

It was feminism, too, that encouraged women to become entrepreneurs when they bumped into what became known as glass ceilings, so that now women are prominent among the founders of new small businesses. By 1984, the US Small Business Administration estimated that there were over three million women business owners in the US, a figure that Jennifer Roback, then a labour economist at Yale, said was nearly double that of 1965.[13] By 1993, it was estimated that six million women had turned their backs on corporate employment to go into business at home.[14]

This positive change in the economic and professional opportunities open to women must have had a positive effect on women's feelings of fulfilment, because so many women took advantage of them. Even the American anti-feminist activist, Phyllis Schlafly, went to school and earned a law degree after her children were born.

Self-Ownership

There are other results of feminism, perhaps less widely obvious, that have clearly had a positive impact on certain groups of women. It was feminists in the 1970s who began to question the age-old assumption, enshrined in law and custom, that women's bodies belonged not to them but to their families, society, or especially their husbands; and to call attention to previously accepted violence against women—wife beating, marital rape, and incest. Although William Blackstone's eighteenth-century *Commentaries on the Laws of England* (which was extremely influential in interpreting Common Law in the US) said that a man had a right to beat his wife with a stick no larger than his thumb, and popular wisdom has preserved such sayings as 'Some women should be beaten regularly, like gongs', there were just no studies of the amount of domestic violence until feminists began calling attention to it. Not only did articles and books begin appearing in the seventies, but feminists began getting changes in the law and protesting police practices that minimised such violence as a family matter and neglected to arrest battering husbands. And it was feminists who invented the concept of shelters for battered wives, and established 1,200 in the US by 1990.[15]

A similar pattern exists with respect to rape. Rape had been widely accepted as a crime caused by sexual deprivation, but feminists succeeded in having it labelled a crime of violence, in instigating training courses for the police who deal with rape victims, and even in changing laws in the US that gave more credence to the testimony of the accused than to the victim. They also protested the laws that, based on Common Law, gave a husband immunity from rape prosecution by his wife, and in 1978, the first US prosecution of a husband for rape occurred in Oregon. The first US conviction in such a case did not occur until 1984 in Florida, and this was a case in which the husband not only punched and beat his wife, bound her hands with tape, cut off her clothes, and tied her arms and legs to the bedposts before raping her, but she was so hurt she had to be taken to a hospital.

Incest was virtually unsuspected as a crime before feminism began to call attention to it, but once the issue was raised, cases began to surface and books began to appear. Men were successfully prosecuted for molesting their daughters, not only based on later adult reports, but on evidence of venereal infections in young children that could only have been caused by sexual activity with an infected adult. There is no question that the phenomenon exists, and is unfortunately not rare.

In 1971, when Bonnie Bluh was travelling in England and Ireland, abortion was illegal in many states in the US There was already a good deal of feminist agitation in the US over the issue, culminating in 1973 in the Supreme Court decision, *Roe v. Wade*, that said a constitutional right to privacy allowed unrestricted abortion in the first trimester. A number of women worldwide have agreed that women should have such a right, and feminists have made this controversy an international issue. The media was riveted by the story of the fourteen-year-old Irish victim of rape who was forbidden to leave the country to get an abortion in 1992, a case that resulted in a change in Irish law, and there are movements to secure a right to abortion not only in the US but in the Catholic Eastern European countries that were formerly Communist.

Again, these legal changes are indicative of a change in social attitudes. No longer was it the case that a man could literally own his wife or his children, as far as the law was concerned. Women subjected to family violence now knew for the first time that outside help was available for them, and they even began to have more choices if they became pregnant. These changes have certainly been large in their effects, and like other earlier feminist changes in society, are beginning to be appreciated in retrospect by many people.

Are Individual Rights Enough?

All of such changes have sprung from a concentration on equality before the law and the plight of individual women denied just treatment in some way. Could it be the case that some women feel that concentrating on them as individuals with rights disparages the family and leaves out the very dreams that Janet Radcliffe Richards said had made them hostile to feminism?

The historian Karen Offen has postulated that two differing focuses have been characteristic of feminism from the beginning, 'two historically distinct and seemingly conflicting modes of argument',[16] which she calls 'individualistic feminism' and 'relational feminism'. Relational feminism, she writes:

> emphasized women's rights as *women* (defined principally by their childbearing and/or nurturing capacities) in relation to men. It insisted on *women's* distinctive contributions in these roles to the broader society and made claims on the commonwealth on the basis of these contributions. By contrast, the individualist feminist tradition of argumentation emphasized more abstract concepts of individual human rights and celebrated the quest for personal independence (or autonomy) in all aspects of life, while downplaying, deprecating, or dismissing as insignificant all socially defined roles and minimizing discussion of sex-linked qualities or contributions, including childbearing and its attendant responsibilities.[17]

Notice in the above quotation that relational feminism 'made claims on the commonwealth'. Relational feminism is not just a movement about gender differences, (although that is one form which is popular, particularly in the social analysis of the anti-pornography movement in Britain and the US today). Relational feminism doesn't just define women in relation to men and children, it often defines them as an interest group that can exercise power to make group claims for benefits.

Instead of an emphasis on individual rights, including the right to physical protection, the emphasis shifts to group rights and the clout to enact a legislative programme to advance women in whatever way seems politically feasible. In many Northern European countries, this clout has resulted in a plethora of entitlements such as child allowances and subsidised day care. Karen Offen says that 'Individualist feminism ... has become increasingly characteristic of British and American discourse since the political philosopher John Stuart Mill published *The Subjection of Women* in 1869 and has reached its most expansive development in twentieth-century Anglo-American thought'.[18] But one 1986 book, *A Lesser Life*, by Sylvia

95

Ann Hewlett,[19] admires the European tradition so much that she criticizes the American feminist movement as too individualist and calls for an alliance between American feminists and organized labour in order to secure such entitlements.

So far, child allowances are not popular in the US, but there is another sign of the influence of relational feminism, a shift from a concern with individual rights to group rights. In a 1992 article in *The Spectator*, Barbara Amiel considers that, to the extent such a shift has occurred, 'the women's movement went off the rails'. She goes on to say:

> It is important to understand that equality for the individual—as in equal opportunity or equality before the law—is a classic liberal ideal, while parity for a group is at best a political and at worst a profoundly reactionary notion. Equality stresses that any qualified human being may become an engineer, plumber, prime minister or jet pilot, regardless of gender, religion or race, while parity maintains that a proportionate number from each group *must* achieve such positions regardless of merit or utility.[20]

Has Feminism Caused Problems for Women?

What impact does this shift, undertaken in the name of feminism, have on women's self-identity and fulfilment? To the extent that individualism and the decisions of individual women opened up opportunities for women and they have taken advantage of it, this certainly has increased fulfilment. But to the extent that such opportunities come as the result of quotas, as Barbara Amiel mentioned, both the *perception* of women's abilities and their self-perception may plummet. After all, self-esteem in the workplace does not come just from *receiving* a job or a promotion; it also comes from feeling that one deserves it, because one is functioning well—that can be hard to feel when those around you consider that you are probably so incompetent that you would not have been hired without government help. If the group is what is important, individuals are more or less interchangeable.

The rise of a concern with group rights may have caused unidentified problems for women's self-esteem, but this has been caused by an abandonment of individualist feminist ideals, not by feminism *per se*. However, there are other specific charges by those hostile to feminism that have some credence. One of these charges is that feminists have given stay-at-home mothers little support or encouragement. This is unfortunately true, even though official feminist publications like *Ms* magazine in the US made a point of saying that they supported housewives as well as working women, since the essence of feminism is choices. Some feminists indeed made it clear that they weren't interested in a woman who had no job or career. Further, the spontaneous economic changes that have occurred have not been kind to would-be housewives. Before a standard of equal-pay-for-equal-work was generally adopted, family men were assumed to be the sole support of their families and earned much more than women, so few women could add much to the family income by going to work. It may well be that the societal shift that has resulted in lower salaries for men and higher for women has put economic pressure on those who would be stay-at-home wives to go into the workplace, because this now would make a real difference to the family's income.

It is hard to believe that any substantial number of women would really like to return to the widespread restriction and dissatisfaction of the feminine-mystique period, even though some who never experienced it might have a sentimental daydream to that effect. It is easy to see the value of living in a previous period if one only concentrates on those aspects one misses in the present, and not on the past details of daily life.

A more sinister criticism of feminism is the idea that feminists have inspired such rage in men that they are responsible for increases in rape and battering. In 1977, the New Hampshire Commission on the Status of Women wouldn't fund shelters for battered wives because, in the words of one commissioner, wives were beaten because 'those women libbers irritated the hell out of their husbands'.[21] Such claims have come, not only from anti-feminists but from some feminists themselves.

> Cultural feminists ... [explain] the recent spread of pornography, and its supposedly more violent nature as part of a male backlash against the women's movement. Threatened by women's demands for greater autonomy, men have reacted defensively and, in response to the magnitude of the perceived threat, sometimes violently. Men wish to re-establish an arrangement ensuring their own uncontested supremacy. From this perspective, both pornography and the alleged

rise in violence towards women are manifestations of the same anti-feminist backlash.[22]

I call this sinister, because there is an implication on the part of the anti-feminists holding this view that these increases (if they are increases in crime and not just in reporting of crime) are somehow justified, and non-criminal acts, no matter how provoking, do not justify criminal acts. In fact, victims of violence are clearly better off as a result of feminist efforts on their behalf. Now at least some attempts are made to help and counsel them in their plight, a welcome change from the years when only the extreme examples of violence caused any comment whatsoever.

Sexual Harassment

But what about sexual harassment? Is it being caused by feminism?

There is some legitimate controversy about the limits of sexual harassment, which is an umbrella term that includes several rather different actions. Cornering women and grabbing parts of their anatomies is a form of battery. Demanding sexual favours in return for jobs, promotions, and academic grades is a form of extortion. Both of these actions should be illegal. There are other reprehensible actions that should certainly be frowned upon, but there is a question as to whether the law or the employer should forbid them—these are the actions usually lumped together as 'creating a hostile or abusive work environment'. Some legal cases pending in the United States as I write this essay are attempting to draw legal definitions in this area that will not conflict with freedom of speech.

This form of harassment is usually used to torment a woman working in an unconventional occupation, or a woman who is seen as a job threat because of her competence, and it is probably true that it has increased with the increasing opportunities for women. If women stayed at home all the time, they wouldn't be sexually harassed in this way. But here again, although the good old stay-at-home days might be nostalgically invoked by a victim of this kind of persecution, sexual harassment wasn't invented today; it was only named. As the American feminist Gloria Steinem said on a talk show, in our youth, 'We called it *life*'. One of the side effects of the television hearings that explored the charges that Anita Hill was harassed by Supreme Court nominee Judge Clarence Thomas was that a number of US politicians and Congressmen reported that their *mothers* told them for the first time of sexual harassment experiences.

Conclusion

The results of the recent feminist movement have been on balance beneficial for women, and enhanced their opportunities and options, but many people still see an emphasis on people as individuals as cold and isolating. Could some aspects of both historical trends within feminism be combined in a way that would be attractive to the average woman? There are moves within feminism in this direction. Some of the most influential voices within feminism that have previously been seen as champions of individualism, for example Betty Friedan, have gone on record as wanting to emphasize a new direction for feminism—one that specifically includes relationships and the family.[23]

Karen Offen herself suggests that although feminism is 'necessarily pro-woman' this does not mean that it is anti-man, and sees its goal as 'a rebalancing between women and men of the social, economic, and political power within a given society, on behalf of both sexes in the name of their common humanity, but with respect for their differences.'[24] She concludes:

> Reintegrating individualistic claims for women's self-realization and choices, with its emphasis on rights, into the more socially conscious relational framework, with its emphasis on responsibilities to others, may provide a more fruitful model for contemporary feminist politics, one that can accommodate diversity among women better than either of the two historical approaches can on their own.[25]

I suggest that the secret for doing this is to stop making 'claims on the commonwealth' in the name of feminism. There is no real conflict between individualist and relational feminism if we have legal equality before the law and individual rights as feminist concerns in the public sphere, and gender differences and relationships and self-fulfilment as feminist concerns in the private sphere, not just for individuals, but for interested social groups. In a society oriented around individual rights, gender differences should not be a concern of the law—they are simply irrelevant. The fact that Western democracies have the freest societies on earth is no reason not to listen to people who would like to make them even better.

Notes

1 Forster, M., *Significant Sisters: The Grassroots of Active Feminism 1839-1939*, 1984, reprint, New York: Alfred A. Knopf, 1985, p. 1. Emphasis in original.

2 Richards, J.R., *The Sceptical Feminist: A Philosophical Enquiry*, 1980, reprint, Boston: Routledge & Kegan Paul, 1982, p. 1.

3 Richards, *op. cit.*, p. 267.

4 Richards, *op. cit.*, p. 284.

5 Mill, J.S. and Mill, H.T., *Essays on Sex Equality*, edited by and with an Introductory Essay by Rossi, A.S., Chicago and London: The University of Chicago Press, 1970, p. 128.

6 See Bluh, B.C., *Woman to Woman: European Feminists*, New York: Starogubski Press, 1974.

7 New York: W.W. Norton & Company, Inc., 1963.

8 Friedan, B., *The Feminine Mystique*, 1963, reprint, New York: Dell Publishing Co., Inc., 1970, p. 12.

9 Taylor, J.K., *Reclaiming the Mainstream: Individualist Feminism Rediscovered*, Buffalo, NY: Prometheus Books, 1992, p. 91.

10 Quoted in Taylor, *op. cit.*, pp. 92-93.

11 Taylor, *op. cit.*, p. 93.

12 Schwartz, F.N., Schiffter, M.H. and Gillotti, S.S., *How to Go to Work When Your Husband Is Against It, Your Children Aren't Old Enough and There's Nothing You Can Do Anyhow*, New York: Simon & Schuster, 1972.

13 See Taylor, J.K., 'The Entrepreneurial Alternative', *Manhattan Report*, Vol. 4, No. 4, 1984, p. 10.

14 Washer, L., 'Home Alone', *Working Woman*, March 1993, p. 46.

15 *Clearinghouse on Women's Issues*, January 1990, quoted in Taylor, *Reclaiming the Mainstream*, p. 134.

16 Offen, K., 'Defining Feminism: a Comparative Historical Approach', *Signs: Journal of Women in Culture and Society*, vol. 4, no. 11, 1988, p. 121.

17 Offen, *op. cit.*, p. 136.

18 Offen, *op. cit.*, p. 135.

19 New York: William Morrow and Company.

20 Amiel, B., 'The Secret Agenda of Gender', *The Spectator*, 17 October 1992, p. 15.

21 Quoted in Taylor, *Reclaiming the Mainstream*, p. 170.

22 Seidman, S., *Embattled Eros: Sexual Politics and Ethics in Contemporary America*, New York: Routledge, 1992, p. 109.

23 See Friedan, B., *The Second Stage*, New York: Summit Books, 1981.

24 Offen, *op. cit.*, pp. 151-52.

25 Offen, *op. cit.*, p. 156.

Other Health & Welfare Unit Publications

The Family: Is It Just Another Lifestyle Choice?, Jon Davies (Editor), Brigitte Berger and Allan Carlson £6.95, 120pp, 1993, ISBN: 0-255 36276-5

Three essays examine the consequences for individuals and for society of the breakdown of the traditional family. They argue that the family is not just another 'lifestyle choice', but vital to Western civilisation.

"The report says that society is paying a heavy price for the belief that the family is just another lifestyle choice." *The Times*

Equal Opportunities: A Feminist Fallacy, Caroline Quest (Editor), *et al.* £6.95, 111pp, June 1992, ISBN: 0-255 36272 2

"Laws banning sex discrimination and promoting equal pay at work damage the interests of women the Institute of Economic Affairs claims today."

The Daily Telegraph

"Let us not above all be politically correct. Let us not become overheated because the Institute of Economic Affairs has brought out a startling report entitled *Equal Opportunities: A Feminist Fallacy.*"

The Times

The Emerging British Underclass, Charles Murray, with Frank Field MP, Joan Brown, Alan Walker and Nicholas Deakin £5.95, 82pp, May 1990, ISBN: 0-255 36263 3

"Britain has a small but growing underclass of poor people cut off from the values of the rest of society and prone to violent, anti-social behaviour." *The Times*

God and the Marketplace, Jon Davies (Editor), *et al.* £4.90, 145pp, 1993 Essays by Rev. John Kennedy, Secretary, Division of Social Responsibility, Methodist Church; Bishop John Jukes, Roman Catholic Bishop of Strathearn; Professor Michael Novak, Professor Richard Roberts, Rev. Simon Robinson

Is capitalism morally acceptable? Theologians representing the Roman Catholic, Anglican and Methodist traditions look at Christian thinking in the light of the collapse of socialism.

"various Christian theologians welcome the economic role of the market and endorse wealth creation as a primary good."

The Daily Telegraph